JAWAHARLAL NEHRU

The Brahman from Kashmir

IMMORTALS OF HISTORY

JAWAHARLAL NEHRU
The Brahman from Kashmir

by Emil Lengyel

FRANKLIN WATTS, INC.
575 Lexington Avenue
New York, N.Y. 10022

Cover photograph courtesy
United Press International

The four lines of poetry on page 200 are from "Stopping by
Woods on a Snowy Evening" from *The Complete Poems of
Robert Frost*. Copyright 1951 by Robert Frost. Reprinted by
permission of Holt, Rinehart and Winston, Inc.

FIRST PRINTING
Copyright © 1968 by Franklin Watts, Inc.
Library of Congress Catalog Card Number: 68-17704
Printed in the United States of America

CONTENTS

JAWAHARLAL NEHRU

The Brahman from Kashmir

Prologue

An endless stream of people was converging on the *maidan,* the marketplace, of the south Indian city of Kanchipuram. They came from long distances to listen to the prime minister of India, Jawaharlal Nehru (jah-*wah*-har-lal *nay*-roo). Affectionately, the people called him *Panditji,* which means the revered scholar. He sat on a platform under the dazzling glare of the floodlights while people kept streaming from all directions: from the city, the neighboring countryside, the coastal mountains of the Ghats, the hill country and the plains, on foot, on bicycles, and by bullock carts. How many of them were assembled? Tens of thousands, perhaps even more. The maidan was large, and it was difficult to guess the size of the crowd in the dusk.

The soft wind wafted in from the Coromandel Coast as the people settled on the parched grass, in the dust, on the tops of the banyan trees. They had come to listen to Panditji, "Mr. India." To many people in the audience he was more than the leader of the country; he was a *rishi,* a superhuman creature, almost a saint. To them, he was able to give protection from the *rakshasas* and *asuras,* the demons and evil spirits filling the nocturnal skies, in the superstitious people's fancy.

1

Panditji stood up, and silence descended upon the assemblage; a silence so profound that the swishing wings of the hawks, frightened out of the peace of their nests in the banyan trees, could be heard.

The klieg lights revealed a man of average height, his chiseled features composed, his face unlined by age. It was a thoughtful face, sometimes sad, sometimes lighted by the flash of a quick smile. He wore the white *khaddar* "Nehru cap," and the tightly buttoned *achkan* tunic.

He was not introduced to the crowd—everybody knew him anyway. Speaking quietly, he stressed his points by accentuating the key words. He spoke in Hindustani, a language of his northern part of India. Most of his listeners spoke Tamil, a language of the south. He talked about his country's second Five-Year Plan, which he expected would raise the living standards by perhaps ten dollars a year per man. The people in the audience listened to him in hushed silence. It made no difference to them that because of the language barrier, they did not understand what he said. In India, there are sixteen major languages, hundreds of minor ones and dialects. Even though the Tamil-speaking people did not grasp his words, they understood his meaning. They would have understood it even if he had been just sitting under the blazing lights, without saying a word. A rishi need not speak to be understood, because wisdom radiates from him and people feel refreshed. It is the same feeling that people have who are cleansed in the sacred waters of the Ganges in Benares, the holy city. The assemblage grasped Nehru's meaning without understanding his words because he had *darshana,* the aura of beatitude. You would not expect Rama, the god, to speak and be understood.

As Nehru spoke in the maidan of Kanchipuram, near the

Coromandel Coast, one would not have sensed the vast difference between his background and that of his audience. They were poor people, mainly illiterate, many diseased. They hoped to receive healing from the white-capped rishi by being exposed to the magic influence of his words.

And Nehru, a member of the highest Hindu caste, educated in the most exclusive schools of Britain, a worldly, highly intelligent statesman—this Nehru felt one with the people and the people felt one with him. He was not only the prime minister of the second most populous nation in the world; he was also the incarnation of his country—"Mr. India."

The aura he had is a quality very few possess. In the Western world, people who have it are called "men of destiny"; they are born leaders who sway the fate of millions. But there are not many who are endowed with such a gift. And it is even rarer for a son with this quality to follow a father who also had it. Yet this was the case of Jawaharlal Nehru.

His father, Motilal, had not lived in an independent India with its own prime minister. He had lived in an India where Britain had ruled as long as men could remember. Motilal had been a man with the aura, a personality commanding religious reverence. He had been one of the first to foresee that times were changing, that relations of the European masters and their Indian subjects were changing, too, and that the time was near when India would be mistress in her own house.

Motilal had been an important person in India, a successful and affluent man. He had jeopardized his social position and his affluence by engaging in a struggle for the freedom of his people—he was one of the pioneers. And people who spoke other languages than his paid attention to him, because they realized that he was an unusual person with great leadership gifts. He never became the leader of the entire country, as his son did, but he was a leader in expressing an ardent national aspiration.

Such great leadership qualities in both father and son are a rare occurrence in history, but there is still another chapter in the story of darshana in the Nehru family.

Jawaharlal Nehru had led his country during the most crucial period of its existence, the period of nation-building, and shortly after his death, India selected his daughter Indira to be the country's leader, the prime minister. The daughter of "Mr. India" became "Mrs. India." She, too, was the type of person that radiated the substance which people recognized as leadership. The meaning of her words was also grasped by people who did not understand her language. They understood her because this third-generation Nehru came from a family with the aura.

This is the life story of Jawaharlal Nehru, the nation-builder, told in the setting of his family. It is the story of a father who played a historic role and a daughter who carried on the work of her family.

∽ ONE ∽

The Brahman from Kashmir

The ancestors of the Nehrus lived in "the dwelling of the gods," the land of Kashmir, in the extreme northwest of India. With its towering mountain peaks, it seems indeed to be the land of the gods. People believed that on those peaks many gods dwelt, their abodes shrouded in mist. They were the gods of Hinduism, the religion observed by most Indians. The Hindu pantheon is filled with divinities, serving every occupation, village, and purpose. How many of those gods had their sanctuaries behind the cloud curtain? Learned men hold that there are forty *crores* of Hindu gods; a tremendous number, because each crore is ten million.

5

Some of the world's highest mountains are in Kashmir. It
has so many peaks of more than 24,000 feet (the tallest peak
in the continental United States, Mount Whitney, is 14,431
feet) that many of them have no names. There are thirty-
three of these giants in Kashmir. The Vale of Kashmir,
deep down below, is a sight for the gods, too. "Wherever
the eye reaches there are verdure and running water," wrote
Emperor Jehangir, a visitor to the vale centuries ago. "The
red rose, the violet, and the narcissus grow of themselves; in
the fields there are all kinds of flowers and all sorts of sweet-
scented herbs. . . ."

Thus, the Nehrus came from the land closest to heaven.
And they belonged to the highest caste, Brahmans (*Brah-
mins*), the priests. As Brahmans, their customs kept them
aloof from everyday people; they were not supposed to have
defiling contact with other castes. They could not dine,
intermarry, or have social dealings with them. If they did,
they would have to undergo purificatory rites.

Below the Brahmans came the Kshatriyas (*Kshat*-tre-yas),
the people who ruled. The merchants, or Vaisyas (*Vise*-yeas),
were the third caste, followed by the Sudras (*Soo*-dras), or
servants, who cleaned houses, tended fields, and performed
other such duties. Those who did not belong to the castes
were called outcastes, or untouchables. They could have no
contact with caste members, and could do only work that was
considered odious by members of castes, such as hauling away
dead animals.

In the eighteenth century, India was inhabited—as it is
today—mainly by Hindus, but there was also a large minority
of another creed. These were the Muslims, believing only
in one god, Allah, and not in forty crores of divinities. It was

not a Hindu, but a Muslim, a member of the Mogul dynasty, who ruled the most important part of India in those days. This was the broad belt of land cradling the Ganges, the Hindus' sacred stream—the country's most fertile and populous area.

A Mogul emperor was the first to discover the Nehru family. Without him, the world may have never heard of this "much blessed" family with the darshana. However, Nehru was not then the family name; it was Kaul, a name quite common in Kashmir.

One day in 1716 the imperial discoverer of the Kauls ascended the mountains on a tour of his land. It was the time of the year when the Red Fort, the historic residence of the Mogul emperors in Delhi on the Jumna River, was enveloped in suffocating summer heat, and the ruler sought relief in the highlands. The emperor was Farrukhsiyar.

In the course of his visit the emperor became acquainted with a youthful Brahman scholar by the name of Raj Kaul. History does not tell how the meeting took place, but it does say that the young scholar found favor in the imperial eyes, and the emperor induced the young man to escort him to Delhi and help him with his administrative tasks at court. Since Kashmiris were generally loath to leave their enchanted land, the emperor must have promised the young man a rich reward.

At Delhi, Raj Kaul was given a *jagir,* an estate, containing several villages and was thus assured a luxurious living at court. He also received a house on the bank of the canal of the river Jumna. In both Persian, the official language of the court, and Urdu, the language of the common people, canal is *nahar.* That word became "Nehru" when people began to refer to the new official's family as Canal-Kauls or Nehru-Kaul. Eventually, the ancestral Kashmiri name was dropped, and the family name became Nehru.

The glory of Pandit Raj Kaul at the imperial court was short-lived, because the reign of his imperial patron was short-lived. The emperor aroused enmity because he was a playboy, spending inordinately long spells of time in the women's quarters—the harem—and the adjacent imperial baths, on the walls of which he had the ecstatic words engraved: "If there is a paradise, this is it, this is it, this is it!"

It was not *it* for long, because on an unparadiselike day a band of noblemen conspirators broke into the imperial harem, found the sovereign in the company of his wives, unceremoniously dragged him out and dumped him into a dungeon. That was the end of Emperor Farrukhsiyar and his well-heeled courtier Nehru.

But the Nehrus must have had something going for them because not long after the demise of their imperial patron, they were reemployed at court. Another member of the family, richly bearded Ganga Dhar, gripping a curved sword and looking fierce, as befitted his station, served as a high police official under the new Mogul emperor.

This Nehru was attached to the court when the Great Mutiny of 1857 broke out. The uprising was directed against the British, the real rulers behind the Mogul throne. In the bloody fighting, countless lives were lost. It took a costly British effort to smash the mutiny and reestablish control. Britain governed the best part of India directly—British India—and the other portion indirectly, the India of the Princes. The princes had authority over their subjects but the British had the final word. After the mutiny, the Nehrus were among the refugees swarming out of the British-occupied capital. The family headed toward one of the best-known places in the world—the city of Agra. Nearby is India's greatest art treasure, the Taj Mahal, the beautiful mausoleum which Shah Jahan had built for Mumtaz Mahal, his favorite wife. So beautifully proportioned is the shrine, that its white marble dome, surrounded by four lacy minarets, seems to float on air against the deep blue background of the Indian sky.

Ganga Dhar Nehru, the fierce-looking police official, died in Agra at the age of thirty-four, four years after the Great Mutiny. Three months after his death, his wife gave birth to a son, who was given the name of Motilal. He was to rise high on the Indian political scene, and he was the first Nehru with the "radiant presence."

The name Motilal reflected the pride of the mother in having borne a son. *Moti* means pearl, and *lal* means ruby. Since Motilal was born after his father's death, he was brought up by Nandlal, the elder of his two brothers. There were also two sisters in the family. Nandlal had built up a large family of his own. He had married at the age of twelve and had two daughters and five sons. Now he had to take care of five others, his mother and younger brothers and sisters—twelve people plus himself and his wife.

Perhaps there was a "blessing" on Nandlal, too, for he did find ways to support his extended family. He started his career by serving as the private secretary of one of the petty Indian princes, Raja Fateh Singh, of the state of Khetri. There were five hundred and sixty-two states in India in those days, some of them comprising a few villages, others with populations as large as America's largest states. Khetri was small, situated in the part of India known as Rajasthan (Country of the Princes). Brother Nandlal must have given a good account of himself because eventually he became the prime minister, head of the *divan,* council of state of his prince. Not only was his title magnificent, but his salary was adequate to support his family. His connections helped him to give his young brother Motilal, a bright youngster, the education available at a princely court. The prince was well disposed toward Motilal, and considered him the right companion for his own children. Young Motilal had vivacious eyes and was literally bursting with energy, a strong indication of his zest for life. There were few sports in India that he did not try, and he distinguished himself in all of them. He was good at cricket and wrestling, but his abiding love was polo.

After his primary education at the court, Motilal was sent to a secondary school in the city of Cawnpore, a trading center on the Ganges. There he saw far more of Indian life than in his small principality. His instructors were British; the language of instruction was English. He was the best student in subjects to which he took a liking, and indifferent in the courses that left him cold. All in all, he gave a good account of himself in his studies, and he particularly distinguished himself by exhibiting a spirit of adventure. "What a pity," an English teacher remarked, "that the boy is not British. He would make an excellent civil servant in the I.C.S. [the Indian Civil Service]."

It was a pity, indeed. However, Motilal was good enough to pass the entrance examination to Muir Central College in Allahabad, the capital of the United Provinces. There he continued to give a reasonably good account of himself. While prone to disperse his energy, he was quick-witted and enterprising.

His secondary school studies completed, Motilal married—

late in life according to Indian standards. He was nineteen, and he married a girl considerably younger than himself. They had a child within a year. The mortality rate in India was tragically high in those days, and especially high among infants. Both Motilal's young wife and their child died shortly after the infant's birth. He was a widower, and hardly out of his teens.

Alone, and not wanting to marry again so soon after his bereavement, Motilal decided to continue his studies. He selected law. A legal degree was good not only for the career of an attorney, but also for other professions, possibly even a governmental job. The higher positions, however, were reserved for the British.

At college Motilal passed his examinations "with drooping colors," as he said jokingly years later. Brains he had enough; energy, more than enough; zest, in abundance; but he was not at his best when not doing the work best suited to his taste. He had not yet found his bearings in law, but he pulled himself together when he approached his bar examination. He passed it with flying colors. He was now a *vakil,* a barrister, qualified to plead cases in all courts, and he was determined to make law his calling.

Appearing in his heavy black-silk gown, the traditional white wig on his dark hair, handsome Motilal Nehru cut an impressive figure. His face with its almost Teutonic square cut was dominated by a high forehead, large in comparison with his angular jaw; his nose was nobly chiseled. The two wings of his carefully tended moustache sloped downward, leaving his high cheekbones unobstructed. His meticulously parted black hair was heavily pomaded. One of his characteristic traits was to clench his fists when presenting his arguments in court, not as a sign of anger, but of mental exertion.

Motilal Nehru's most revealing features were his eyes.
They betrayed his moods and were, it was said, "the home of
a thousand little demons" when reflecting a jocular temper,
or the incubator of tempests when his anger exploded. He
could be a most engaging companion as well as a ruthless
adversary. His mind was rapierlike, and he had the capacity
to wrap himself completely in the cases he pleaded. To him
a court case was work—arduous work—but it was also a
mission: he represented truth; his adversary, falsehood. He
had to believe in the cases he tackled, and when he did he
was invincible.

At twenty-two, he was far more mature than his contemporaries in the Western world. People matured more quickly
on the Indian subcontinent than in the West. It did not take
long before prospective clients recognized the young vakil's
qualities. They realized that in spite of his youth, he had the
knack of reaching the core of contentious issues, and that his
dazzling intellect enabled him to present it effectively to the
judges. People began to talk about his skill, and soon he did
not need to look for clients. They were looking for him.

Allahabad was an unusually appropriate place for a brilliant young barrister, since it was one of the four cities in
India with a high court. The judges were Britishers, and they
were the best of their kind. Britain could maintain itself
on the subcontinent only by dispensing impartial justice. The
brilliant law lords were also good judges of the barristers
pleading cases. There was no practicing vakil who appealed
to them more than the youthful Motilal Nehru. The chief
judge of the Allahabad High Court, Sir Grimwood Mears,
attributed Motilal's preeminence in his profession to a profusion of gifts. "Knowledge," the learned judge said, "came

easily to Motilal Nehru and as an advocate he had the art of presenting his case in its most attractive form. Every fact fell into its proper place in the narration of the story and was emphasized in just the right degree. He had an exquisite public speaking voice and a charm of manner which made it a pleasure to listen to him."

The judge, naturally, could speak only of the impression which Motilal made when at court. He could not know that at home the barrister with the charming manner occasionally exploded in towering rages of temper. Motilal could not put up with sloth, dishonesty, stupidity, or inefficiency.

The young barrister could easily support a family, and he married again when he was twenty-two. His bride was called Swaruprani (Beauty Queen), and the name of her family was Thussu. They, too, had descended from the mountainous world of Kashmir, and they, too, were Brahmans. The new home of the Thussus was the city of Lahore. At the time of Swaruprani's marriage to Motilal, she was fifteen.

Swaruprani was frail, like a porcelain figurine, with small feet and hands. She had a pleasant oval face in which her eyes looked inordinately large. They were not as luminous and vivacious as those of the Nehrus, but were sad and questing. Her pitch-black hair was parted in the middle as meticulously as that of her husband. While Motilal dressed as an English gentleman, the Beauty Queen wore the traditional garb of well-to-do Hindu women, beautifully embroidered saris of substantial texture. While Motilal exuded strength, his wife was of delicate health.

Everything seemed to be going well for Motilal, when suddenly there was a new crisis. His brother, Nandlal, died, and the burden of supporting his large family fell to Motilal.

Luckily, he was doing so well that he could assume the additional burden without hardship. Then another great sorrow came—the child born to Swaruprani died. In the India of those days it was a near-miracle for a baby to survive.

Motilal Nehru's changes of address in Allahabad indicate his success in his profession. His first home was in the heart of the city itself, the capital of the United Provinces, the core of British India, so filled with people as to be bursting at the seams.

The city was close to the center of India's great food basket, the plains of the sacred Ganges River, at the point where another hallowed stream, the Jumna, joined it. Allahabad was an administrative, educational, and, above all, a religious center that attracted countless people to its sacred shrines. It had been named the City of Allah, or Allahabad, during the Muslim Mogul dynasty. Although it had a sizable Muslim population, the majority was Hindu.

The juxtaposition of religions was typical of India—Hindu majority and Muslim minority. In some locations, especially in the northwest and northeast, the order was reversed—Muslim majority and Hindu minority. The inability of Muslim and Hindu to live together peacefully was the greatest problem of the country.

It was in the old city of Allahabad that a son was born to Motilal and Swaruprani. They called the infant Jawaharlal (Ruby Jewel). The date of his birth was November 14, 1889. Years later, when Jawaharlal Nehru was famous, he liked to mystify people by saying that the year of his birth was 1946. That was true, reckoning according to the Samvat calendar, which was widely used in India at the time. The Samvat is fifty-seven years ahead of the Gregorian calendar, which is now in general use. The year 1 on the Samvat

(57 B.C. on the Gregorian) is the first year of the reign of the legendary King Vikramaditya, "Sun of Power."

The birth of a boy to the Nehrus caused much rejoicing. A boy could work and become a breadwinner. There would be no need of a dowry for the later marriage—and who but the rich could carry the cost of a lavish wedding? But above all, a boy was a blessing because he could carry on the family traditions, and set the torch to the funeral pyre of the deceased father, ensuring a better fate in future life. The joy in the Nehru house was particularly great because the newborn infant seemed to be a robust little fellow, with lung power that shook the house. He had a pair of eyes that attracted instant attention—coal black and unusually vivacious.

"Look at those eyes," his kinsmen exclaimed. "Look how luminous they are." And, indeed, they were full of light.

"Just like the eyes of Lord Krishna," a devout relative commented.

"They are mischievous eyes," another said, "and show unusual brains."

Then the usual family game began, the game of comparisons. The child resembled the father, some relatives declared; he had the eyes "with the thousand little demons." He resembled the mother, another kinsman said; he had her oval face and beautiful features. Finally, the relations agreed that he had something of both the mother and father; and that the baby was supremely bright, like the Lord Krishna; and beautiful to behold, like the Lord Rama. They also agreed that the horoscope the sage had cast for the marriage of Motilal and the Beauty Queen must have been auspicious.

It was auspicious, indeed, because the child survived his first year, crucial for Indian babies. He survived the second and third years, too. And at the end of the third year Motilal made a decision which would greatly affect the life of the boy. He sold his house in the crowded center of Allahabad and moved westward toward the Civil Lines, where the British officials resided. Between the outskirts of the city and the Civil Lines was an area inhabited by well-to-do Indians. There, the houses were not crowded together, and each had a garden of its own. It was an area without swarms of people jostling in the streets. Vakil Motilal Nehru was rich enough now to buy a large house at 8 Elgin Road, between the city proper and the Civil Station. The city, to the east, was typical of India with its historic traditions, its clamor, scents, sicknesses, and religious festivals. A few hundred yards westward was Little England, the Civil Station, with the pink-cheeked British officials of the I.C.S. leading the social life of another world. They read *The Times* of London, played cricket, attended services in English churches, ate English food, drank English drinks, dressed for dinner, were attended by swarms of servants, worried about promotions, talked about the long-awaited vacation trips to England and about the education of their children.

Between the busy city and the sedate Civil Station, the East and West came within nodding distance. The Nehrus' move was an important stage in their life. By moving to the Elgin Road residence, Motilal Nehru indicated that he wanted his son to be brought up in the atmosphere of the British world. Also, he wanted to come as close to the British way of life as the social rules permitted. He would have moved *into* the Civil Station, if that had been possible. However, it was not possible for native Indians, no matter how distinguished or well-to-do they were.

Motilal Nehru had by now become the most fashionable barrister of northern India. His clients were some of the most

prominent people of the land, maharajas and business tycoons
—some of them fabulously rich. Motilal kept gaining more
authority in the courts. He not only had zest, industry,
persistence, and dynamic presence, but he also had universal
respect. The judges came to realize that cases entrusted to
Motilal were nearly always important ones. He manifested
the qualities Indians associate with the "magic presence."
Motilal Nehru was described as a "unique personality," a
"roaring torrent," a "doughty warrior," the "uncrowned
king." And he became richer every year.

Eventually he became rich enough to acquire the most expensive mansion in Allahabad, at 1 Church Road, and he
called it Anand Bhawan, Abode of Bliss. It was in that house
that Jawaharlal grew to manhood, and there he became
acquainted with the great wealth of India—for the few—
and the incredible poverty—for the many. Today the house
on Church Road is a historic monument.

The house was even closer to the Civil Station than the
Nehrus' previous home. Jawaharlal was eleven in 1900, when
the family moved into the new place. His sister Swarup was
born there that year, and another sister, Krishna, seven years
later.

Anand Bhawan was comparatively large even by the
standards of the land of the great palaces of the maharajas.
The mansion was multistoried, with high-ceilinged rooms,
furnished in a regal way. The furniture was mahogany and
teak; the tapestry was from Persia, the glassware from
Venice, and the chinaware from Dresden, the most exquisite
product of that German city so famous for its porcelain.
This ultramodern house of northern India had running water
—a novelty then—and was wired for electricity, an even
greater novelty. Indeed, Motilal's house was the first in all

of Allahabad to have electric lights. The floors were surrounded by spacious verandas in the shadow of overhanging
balconies, with a covered pergola on the top. Filigreed
masonry protected the dwellers from the glare of the summer
sun. The house also had more than a dozen bathrooms.

The grounds that Motilal had acquired with the mansion
were no less luxurious than the house. Throughout the entire
year one could enjoy exotic flowers and inhale their heavy
fragrance. The area was spacious enough for banyan trees,
whose intertwined limbs provided shade for protection on
sultry summer days. There was also an indoor swimming
pool.

The senior Nehru had a stable full of glossy black mares,
famous in the region. But he was a modern man, too. As
soon as the first horseless carriages appeared in the Western
world, he acquired several. Indeed his was the first auto-
mobile that Allahabad had ever seen. He bought it on a
European trip in 1904. The roads in those days were poor
even in western Europe, let alone in India. But Motilal
kept buying new cars to replace the older ones. The prestige
cars at that time were the Italian Fiat and Lanza, and they
were the ones Nehru bought. They were the talk of the town.
Nehru practiced what the American social thinker Thorstein
Veblen has called "conspicuous consumption."

Motilal Nehru was a rare specimen of man in more than
one respect. He liked to tinker with gadgets, install bells, experiment with lights, and introduce the latest technical
appliances in house and garden, even though he had a swarm
of servants. So large was the number of domestics that
Motilal sometimes thought of taking a census of them. New
faces popped up endlessly. Old hands helped greenhorn kinsfolk to find places in the rich vakil's home. There were so

many of them that they ran out of space for additional sleeping bunks. What matter? The newcomers slept under the banyan trees.

There were many resident relatives in the house, too. Kinsmen just dropped in, stayed a while, then moved on. One could not shut the door in a kinsman's face. Besides nieces and nephews and their offspring, there were countless cousins, often generations removed.

But even though the house was crowded, Jawaharlal grew up a lonely boy. For eleven years he had no sister and he could not play with city children, who lived in a different world. Nor could he play with the British children in the Civil Station. They, too, lived worlds apart from him. Besides, Jawaharlal liked to keep to himself, reading and daydreaming. His father was a very busy man. "He [his father] seemed to me the embodiment of strength and courage and cleverness," Jawaharlal was to say years later, "far above all the other men I saw and I treasured the hope that when I grew up I would be rather like him."

From his father he learned many things, and particularly the desire to work and to excel. It was from Motilal that the boy learned: "A moment lost in idleness can never be retrieved." And this: "Every moment has to be lived intensely. At the end of each day a man must ask, 'What have I done, useful or otherwise, during the past day?'" While Jawaharlal admired his father, he could not get close to him in his early youth because Motilal's practice kept growing, keeping him busy all the time. The gap between the "uncrowned king" and his shy son was too great. His father was more like a god to him than a man.

Yet, the Abode of Bliss was not a monotonous place, for Motilal was the center of a busy social life. Sometimes his laughter shook the house, while at other times his wrath erupted into family tempests. The case of the missing pen was an illustration of the latter mood.

At the time, Jawaharlal was still young and could not understand why his father should have two pens when he could write only with one. Yet, there were two pens on his father's desk. At least, there were two pens for a while, and then there was only one.

Motilal noticed the disappearance of one pen and wanted to know its whereabouts. In search of the missing item, he had the house turned upside down. Even the belongings of the servants were searched, yet the pen was not found.

Then one day it was found in the possession of the son. A cornered lion could not have emitted a more shattering roar than Motilal. Even though the Abode of Bliss had been built to resist earthquakes, its very rafters were shaking when the pen was found. During the next few minutes, the Abode of Bliss became the Abode of Pain, and it remained such for days. It took that much time before young Jawaharlal could sit down.

What of the relations between mother and son? She was kind as only mothers know how to be. But at that time women were not prepared to be the intellectual equals of men. The Beauty Queen was far more at home in household affairs than in matters of interest to the boy—history, the Hindu classics, and books about far-off lands.

Yet, Jawaharlal did have contact with the outside world. He was introduced to it by a *munshi,* a scribe of his father's. White-bearded Mubarak Ali, a kindhearted man, was a Muslim, but he introduced the young boy to the Hindu sacred writs, too.

First, the munshi acquainted him with the enchanted land

of the Ramayana, the story of the divine Rama of royal
blood. Some thirty centuries before the Christian era, a powerful family, the Kosalas, ruled in India. They were a heroic
breed that produced Rama, for whom the epic was named.
He was as brave and attractive as only gods could be. At that
time, there was another great family in the land, the Videhas,
headed by King Janaka, whose daughter was the enchanting
Princess Sita. The king wanted the best man to win his
daughter's hand, and he arranged a set of tests for the
contenders, probing not only their physical but also their
moral fiber. Lord Rama won the tests, thus becoming Sita's
spouse. But evil minds, filled with spite, sought to thwart
the happiness of the divine couple. Enemies arose on all sides,
and from the peak of happiness, Rama and his beloved Sita
descended into the vale of tears. Rama was exiled and Sita
kidnapped by Ravana, the demon king. Eventually, Rama
subdued his foes and became the king, loving his people and
being loved by them. Even though new trials barred the way
of happiness, he did not abandon hope.

> As a father to his children to his loving men he
>   came,
> Blessed our homes and maids and matrons till our
>   infants lisped his name.
> For our woes and troubles Rama hath the ready tear
> To our humble tales of suffering Rama lends his
>   willing ear.

The Muslim munshi also introduced the Brahman boy into
the intricacies of the other Hindu epic, the Mahabharata. It
acquainted Jawaharlal with a different type of world, the
world of men at war. The highlight of this epic is the

Bhagavad-Gita, the Song of the Blessed Lord Krishna, which
has been compared with the Sermon on the Mount. This is
the song of the Divine Krishna on the eve of a major battle
between two clans, and it contains some of the most important precepts of the Hindu religion, among them the obligation to do one's duty. "Do your duty under all circumstances,"
Lord Krishna admonished the warrior Arjuna on the eve of
a crucial battle. By doing one's duty, one carried out a sacred
obligation. Krishna enjoined the warrior to bear in mind that
while bread was essential for the body, spiritual values were
indispensable for life. Salvation was achieved by placing
one's trust in the Lord Krishna. "Fill thy heart with Me, be
thou devoted to Me." Through such devotion one established
communion with the invisible universe.

Even though Motilal was of the priestly caste, he did not
practice his religion. Not that he was irreligious, but he
considered ethics, not rituals, the substance of man's noblest
creed. So Jawaharlal learned about the basic tenets of his
Hindu religion not from his father but from Mubarak Ali,
the non-Hindu.

Jawaharlal learned that a man's duty was prescribed by his
caste. Life to the Hindu had no clear-cut beginning and end
—birth and death—and was merely a station in an endless
pilgrimage. The newborn child had had another reincarnation before his birth, as a man, animal, or inanimate object.
After "death" there was another life. This was the doctrine
of reincarnation, or *samsara*. Only a few privileged people
were exempted from the endless succession of lives. Their
lives ended in *nirvana,* the absolute end, without reincarnation, the bliss of endless sleep.

As for the four hundred million gods, the entire universe
was filled with them, and earthly life was the mirror of the

gods' abode. To injure any manifestation of nature would be to injure these gods, too. Man's obligation was to respect the reflection of the god-filled world.

At the time that young Jawaharlal became acquainted with the tenets of his religion through his father's scribe, he had only vague ideas about the real nature of his creed. "Of religion I had hazy notions. To me it seemed a woman's affair. Father and my older cousins treated the question humorously and refused to take it seriously. The women of the family indulged in various ceremonies and I rather enjoyed them, though I tried to imitate to some extent the casual attitude of the grown-up men of the family."

Allahabad was then a religious center for the Hindus (as it is today) and there young Nehru became acquainted with another phase of Indian life, unknown at home—the pilgrimage.

How had Allahabad become a sacred place to the pilgrims? It all went back to the time when the gods and the demons were wrestling for a jug of nectar hidden in the sacred waters of the Ganges. The jug contained the nectar of immortality, and it was concealed at the confluence of three rivers: the Ganges, the mighty river of the Hindustan plains; the Jumna, which flows by the city of Delhi, the capital of India then and now; and a third river, not on the map and not seen by human eyes. It is visible only to the gods and it has no name. At the point where the three rivers meet, the Hindus have their sacred place of pilgrimage—Allahabad, the city of Allah.

The fight between the gods and the demons ended with victory for the gods, and thus they gained immortality. While wrestling for the jug, however, a drop of the nectar fell on the soil of what would become Allahabad. The city became an immortal place, the gods' abode, where millions of people converged during the Kumbh Mela—"jug festival." Three other cities have smaller melas of their own.

At the time of the mela, pilgrims from all over the Indian world converge on Allahabad at the confluence of the three rivers. A dip in those waters is supposed to wash away sin, assuring a blissful future life. So frantic is the rush of the faithful into the water that sometimes hundreds of worshipers are trampled underfoot.

From a distance, young Jawaharlal observed the mela while his father's munshi showed him the pilgrims' quarters, mostly in the open fields, in the alleyways, in the gutters. There he saw the India he did not see in the Abode of Bliss—the India where starvation was endemic and where death by famine was not considered important enough to be reported in the press. There he saw the myriads who lacked even rags to cover their bodies. This was his introduction to the real India.

The lonely boy in the Abode of Bliss had contact with Indian life in other ways, too. He saw his native land on its festival days of joy and sorrow. India has many festivals that help people to forget their everyday lives. Without them life would be less worth living.

It was again his father's elderly scribe who introduced the boy to the lighter side of life. The follower of Islam showed him the feasts of his own creed and of the Hindu majority.

Jawaharlal learned that most of the festivals were linked to the farmer's calendar—the seeding of the land, the harvest, the monsoons, the fertility-producing periodic rains.

Jawaharlal shared the love of his fellow Indians for the gay festivities of the *holi*, a fertility rite in honor of Lord

Krishna. Fertility in the mind of the farmer was linked with life-giving water, and thus the source of the holy rites was a wish for a prosperous life. The water used on that day was squirted on friends with much gaiety.

Young Jawaharlal also liked the other great Hindu festival of fertility, *dewali,* honoring the goddess Kali, who fought evil demons. The faithful helped her by setting up countless twinkling lights in shrines and temples, on the roofs of houses and huts, and under the trees. The Hindus besought the goddess to provide food and avert famine. The boy also celebrated the end of the monsoon season by the festival of *dusserah,* when masked dancers in the streets acted out the parable of the god's triumph over evil, and *chokras* (urchins) frolicked under the cloudless sky. Like so many others, Jawaharlal was partial to the festivals honoring Lord Krishna. Most important of these was the *janamasthami,* the celebration of his birth, which had taken place in a dungeon. The celebration began at midnight. Jawaharlal would have liked to await the god's arrival on earth but his eyelids became heavy with sleep.

Jawaharlal also liked the Kashmir festivals brought from the mountains, the abodes of gods. His particular favorite was Navoroz, the New Year, when food from the hills was eaten.

But the greatest holiday for young Jawaharlal was his own birthday. He received many presents and became the family hero for a day, almost as if he had been Lord Krishna himself. He had only one complaint about that day—he would have liked to have more than one a year. The time was to come when he wished there had been only one birthday in many years.

The family munshi also introduced the boy to the festivities of Islam. Most important of these was Ramadan, the "fast-feast," in memory of Allah's handing the Koran, the Sacred Writ, to the prophet Muhammad. Ramadan was the month during which the munshi's coreligionists had to fast during the day. But during the dark hours they could feast— that is, those who could afford it could do so. During those hours, the gaiety was boundless. Another Muslim festival that fascinated the boy was the Muharram, in memory of the deaths of the prophet's successors in the distant past.

Even a less observant boy than Jawaharlal would have noticed two of the most prominent facts of life in India during his visits to town for these festivals. One of them was the "two souls" of his native land as represented by its two most important religions, Hinduism and Islam. They were not merely two creeds but two ways of life—Hinduism with its four hundred million gods, and Islam with its one god, Allah. The consequences of these two different creeds were too obvious for the bright boy to overlook. Hindus and Muslims worshiped in different clothes, had different customs, went to different schools (if they went to school at all), and had different heroes. They had different traditions, and marked different episodes in history. In fact, even though they were neighbors, they lived worlds apart.

Did the two "communities" live together in peace? Jawaharlal thought so. The family scribe was a Muslim and the boy considered him a second father, whom he saw more frequently than his own parent. On their visits to Allahabad, the old man introduced the boy to his Muslim friends, who could not do enough for him. These Muslims in town either lived in clusters of houses or were dispersed among the Hindus. They were close neighbors and yet they lived differently. The boy did read about communal strifes that had resulted in bloodshed, and thus he realized that there was a "communal problem." But most of the time the problem was far away, and Allahabad saw almost nothing of it.

Had the scribe and Jawaharlal's mother not taken him to the religious festivals, he might have thought that most Indian houses were like his, with a swimming pool, a garage, and droves of domestic servants. But he became acquainted with the real India during his visits to other quarters, and Indian reality made him sad.

He saw starving Indians in the center of the city, holding out trembling hands for a pittance, without which they might die overnight. Their dead bodies were collected by street cleaners in the morning. Jawaharlal talked to the scribe about these tragic events. The old man listened and then tried to explain the sad facts of Indian life. Yes, he told the boy, there was poverty in India, and also starvation. The government and the princes tried to relieve the poverty by tapping the Ganges and the Indus for irrigation. But the power of the gods was not in their hands. Sometimes the monsoon was inadequate or it failed altogether, and famine struck the land. What could frail man do against Allah's will?

The abysmal poverty was also the people's fault because they had larger families than they could afford. Jawaharlal saw that they lived in filth, breeders of plagues. Every year millions died of malaria. The scribe told the boy that since he could do nothing about this, he should not become saddened.

Jawaharlal listened with close attention. But one evening, after a particularly heartbreaking trip to town, he obtained his father's permission to go to bed without supper. He could not force himself to eat. His father was surprised at the request, but attached no particular importance to it, and started to prepare his court cases for the next day. Then, suddenly, he thought of Jawaharlal's strange conduct. Leaving his briefs, he rushed to his son, and found him in his room on the bare floor. This was the boy's way of expressing his sympathy for the poor people. Motilal was moved, and decided to pay more attention to the preoccupations of his son.

But Jawaharlal's home environment was nothing like the average Indian's hut, for Motilal Nehru wanted to live the life of rich Britishers. He had his clothes made on Savile Row, London's famous men's tailoring center. The heavy gold chain of his watch across his Scotch-tweed vest bespoke affluence. Every morning *The Times* of London was on his breakfast table. With his bowler hat and the umbrella he carried in the monsoon season, he was the picture of the fashionable English barrister. The slight "tan" on his face could have been acquired at the English seacoast.

He spoke faultless English, and his liquor cabinet was stocked with British imports. There were Englishmen, as well as Indians, at his parties, and the Indian guests were wealthy fellow-barristers and the richest men in town. The roster of the Englishmen visiting the Nehru mansion represented the top section of the Indian Civil Service, the people who ruled India. The white steeds of the coach belonging to the governor, the highest official of the province, were often seen in front of the Abode of Bliss. The governor ruled some forty million people, more than the population of Britain then. Among the Nehrus' visitors were the commissioners, heads of the divisions of the large administrative units. Each of these officials ruled over millions. Some officials had intriguing titles, such as "collector" in charge of districts —so called because their predecessors collected taxes when the land was governed by the British East India Company, a private corporation. Other visitors in the Nehru house were district officers, the D.O.'s, a select body of officials that constituted the country's administrative backbone.

The English visitors enjoyed the good times in the Nehrus' home. They liked the food, the drinks, the luxurious service, the elegant mansion and, above all, the cordiality of the host, his stories, and the stories of his court cases, which he embellished so well that they sounded like tales from the *Arabian Nights.*

Yet, in spite of all this, a gulf separated Motilal from the British. As an Indian, he was barred from many conveniences his guests had. In spite of all his prominence and affluence, he could not, for instance, ride in a first-class train coach— forbidden to "natives," and carrying the sign, *For Europeans Only.*

He could have paid the highest fees of the most exclusive clubs, but they too were for Europeans only. Benches in public parks often displayed the same sign. Thus, although the British cultivated social relations with people like Motilal and lived off the country, the gulf between the people could not be bridged. The British were considered superiors, the Indians inferiors.

The gulf was in evidence when Jawaharlal's education was under discussion. The schools for "natives" were not considered good, and the boy, therefore, had to have a European tutor. The choice finally fell on a many-sided young scholar, Ferdinand T. Brooks.

Brooks, born under the British flag on a steamer bound for

South America, was the son of a Scottish-Irish father and a
French-speaking Belgian mother. At the time Motilal discovered Brooks, the young man's father had a civil service
job at Allahabad.

Of importance in the selection was the fact that young
Ferdinand was a theosophist. A new movement then, theosophy had been popularized by a remarkable English woman,
Annie Besant. The translation of the Greek word—wisdom
of God—supplies only a partial explanation of its essence.
Theosophists strove to be filled with the wisdom of God,
which they expected to be revealed to them in flashes of
insight while they were engrossed in the profound contempla-
tion of eternal verities. God's wisdom would lead them to
their ultimate aim—to lead a virtuous life, pleasing to God,
and useful to fellow humans.

Annie Besant, the leading theosophist, sought to achieve
this aim by turning to the wisdom of India, reflected in its
sacred writings, especially the Bhagavad-Gita. According to
her interpretation, the wisdom of India and of theosophy
endeavored to give supremacy to the spirit over the call of the
flesh. She considered material values insignificant when
compared with man's peace of mind.

Although Motilal was not a religious Hindu, he was for
a time attracted to this substitute for religion. He may have
felt compensated by the doctrine for the treatment accorded
to Indians by the British. The theosophists considered Indians
superior to the people of the West, who were thought to
be mired in gross materialist ways.

Ferdinand Brooks was highly regarded in the Nehru household because he was an inspiring teacher, a one-man faculty.
Jawaharlal Nehru was never to forget him. The tutor was
adept in both natural and social sciences. He transformed the

basement of the Abode of Bliss into a laboratory where teacher and pupil carried out chemistry and physics experiments.

The teacher inspired his pupil to discover the world through books. He introduced him to the lower depths of life in England through the novels of Dickens, to the English upper-class life through the novels of Thackeray, and to England's Middle Ages through the novels of Scott. Nehru was also attracted to fantasies, social satire, romantic stories about fairy-tale countries, and detective stories, among them such works of H. G. Wells as *The Invisible Man* and *The Time Machine.* He was enthralled by Lewis Carroll's *Alice in Wonderland* and Anthony Hope's *Prisoner of Zenda.* His special favorite was a contemporary best seller, Jerome K. Jerome's *Three Men in a Boat.* And for a time he could not read enough of Sherlock Holmes.

In those days, there was no reason why young Jawaharlal should not have been content with his life. The son of a rich and respected father, his home life, although quiet, was harmonious. But for years he had been the only child in a spacious house, living between two worlds, British and Indian, but in neither of them. Sensitive, his loneliness became harder for him to bear with each year.

Britain's might seemed unshakable in those days. But it was shaken in far-off South Africa by simple farmers of Dutch descent, calling themselves Boers. They had established two small republics, Transvaal and the Orange Free State, adjacent to British-held land. Vast finds of gold and diamonds in the two republics started the English on a policy of expansion against their neighbors, and at the turn of the century a war erupted.

The world expected the British to steamroller the Boers

into instant submission. That, however, did not happen, and the two small republics held their own. It took two years for the British to subdue the Boers, and the victory was costly. The resistance of the Dutch was so impressive that the British felt impelled to accord self-government to them.

The Boer War was an eye-opener for many people in India, and especially for Motilal Nehru. If small groups of farmers came close to defeating the British, could not hundreds of millions of Indians do the same, especially since there were so few Englishmen in India's Civil Stations? Motilal's son, politically mature for his age, also took notice of the situation.

Shortly thereafter, another event shook the world. Again, it was a war, this time in the Far East, and the antagonists were the Russians and the Japanese. The Russians had a global empire, one-sixth of the land surface of the world, while the Japanese had a small island realm which the Russians could have tucked into a tiny corner of their country. Everybody expected the Russians to crush Japan. Instead, the Japanese were victorious.

"I remember well," Nehru wrote years later, "how excited I used to get when news came of the Japanese victories." One day he read in the papers about one of the most decisive engagements in the war, a naval battle in the Tsushima Straits in May, 1905. The Japanese Admiral Heihachiro Togo scored a decisive victory over the Russian fleet. This time young Nehru was fully aware of the political significance of the event.

Up to that time, Europeans had been thought to be superior to Asians, and white men stronger than non-whites. Yet the Japanese, who were Asian and non-white, had defeated the Russian whites. This was an exhilarating thought to Indians, and the Nehrus' spirits rose. Could not the Indians do to the British-European whites, what the Japanese had done to the Russians?

The Nehrus were not the only people entertaining such thoughts. There were other people in India, too, who began to think about a free India, not ruled by outsiders. They were thinking about an India in which the *For Europeans Only* sign was not displayed, and in which Civil Stations were not reserved for the ruling race. These were bold thoughts, indeed, for an age in which British rule in India was as much taken for granted as were the sun, the moon, and the unchangeable order of the stars.

∽ TWO ∾

Education in England

The S.S. *Macedonia* of the Peninsular and Oriental Steam
Navigation Company weighed anchor on May 13, 1905, in
the harbor of Bombay, majestic gateway of India. It was a
torrid day, as mid-May days are likely to be in that tropical
country. Silently the vultures circled under the leaden sky,
swooping down upon the nearby Tower of Silence, the open-
air burial ground of the Parsees, members of a religious sect
who disposed of the bodies of their dead by exposing them to
birds of prey. A cloud of quarrelsome gulls followed the
ship, apparently able to distinguish between luxury liners,

which released large amounts of waste, and vessels of emigrants, from which the pickings were slim.

The Nehru family, headed by Motilal, was on board. The senior Nehru looked more majestic than ever, and more than ever like an Englishman. Swaruprani looked very Indian in her gold-embroidered sari. Jawaharlal, now sixteen and mature for his age, was impeccably dressed in the fashion of the upper-class Englishman. In adolescence, young Nehru's eyes were no less luminous than in his earliest youth. Now he was looking at the receding Indian shoreline with a wistful smile. Also aboard was his little sister, Swarup, a beautiful, vivacious child, now five years old. Nan, as the family called her, became the pet of the ship. Domestic servants accompanied the family on the long voyage to the west.

The wistful look on Jawaharlal's face was his farewell to his native land, which he was not to see again for years. From a distance, the Bombay waterfront looked celestial. Young Nehru was going to Britain for the education of an upper-class English boy. He had wanted this trip and yet now he felt the pangs of separation. He thought with nostalgia of his homeland's tropical climate, of her marble gateway, and even of the Tower of Silence.

What did he expect to find in England? He expected to find *himself* through the best available schools. He wanted to move from the Abode of Bliss into the Abode of Knowledge, from which he could enter life. Although the British were the masters of his country, he did not dislike them, in spite of those signs that said For Europeans Only. He was headed now for a country where there were no such signs. In Britain, he, the Hindu Brahman, was to be a "European," too.

Young Nehru wanted to see the British at home, to live with them, learn from them and to see, above all, what filled them with self-confidence and gave them their strength. How could a tiny country such as England rule over India, a subcontinent? He wanted to penetrate into the secrets of the British way of life. Was it their schools and the knowledge they acquired that gave them their strength? Or was it their traditions, their history, their social, political, and economic systems?

For days the steamer cleaved the waters of the Arabian Sea, as leaden as the tropical sky. On board, the Nehrus met distinguished Britishers of the upper classes. There were no *For Europeans Only* signs, and there was apparent equality in the luxury cabins.

For weeks they traveled. They stopped at Aden, at the entrance of the Red Sea; at Port Said, entrance gate of the Suez Canal; at Malta, a fueling spot in the Mediterranean; and at Gibraltar, symbol of the rocklike quality of Britain's imperial might. Then they emerged into the Atlantic Ocean, its wrathful green waters smashing angrily against the hull of the ship, as though resentful of the intrusion.

Finally, they reached London, wrapped in gloom, the gray of the northern climate whipped by rushing rains from the Gulf. The trying climate may have accounted for the British strength, Jawaharlal thought. Who but the strongest could endure it?

The Nehrus took a suite in one of the most elegant London hotels, where a member of the House of Lords was their neighbor, and little Nan's happy chatter established the closest contact between the Englishman and the Indian family. The goal of the family, however, was not London, but a small town northwest of the capital. This was Harrow, site of the famous school where young Jawaharlal was to obtain his education.

Harrow's public school, the English equivalent of American private schools, was, with Winchester and Eton, one of the most exclusive secondary schools in Britain. The three were considered incubators of scholastic excellence. In existence for centuries, Harrow had nurtured such British immortals as Palmerston, Lord Byron, and Winston Churchill.

Nehru had read about his future alma mater, and was thrilled by its landmarks, especially St. Mary's-Church-on-the-Hill. At first sight, it seemed to float on a verdant sea of boughs. The sixteenth-century school was majestic, some of its classrooms having been in use for centuries. Surrounding it was the lovely English countryside, so different from Allahabad's setting. Here it was bursting with life, trees, grass, flowers, houses, and public buildings. Everything was in its place, in just the right proportion, in the right perspective, as picturesque as if designed by master artists, with a surprise at every meandering turn of the road. In India, the cows, scrawny and venerated, roamed everywhere. Here, fat and placid, they grazed behind protecting fences, parts of the picturesque landscape.

It was through his connections and prestige that Motilal had enrolled his son in the exclusive school. It had not been easy because few places were available for Indians. After their arrival at Harrow, the Nehrus' first call was on the headmaster, Dr. Joseph Wood, a highly learned man who was to supervise the boy's studies. Jawaharlal's tutor was another scholar, Dr. Edgar Stogdon, who was to become the vicar of famed St. Mary's-on-the-Hill.

It took only a few days for Jawaharlal to assume the Harrovian look—gray flannels, blue jacket, and straw hat. By way of quick adjustment to his environment, he promptly acquired a cricket bat for Britain's national sport. In Britain, the Eton-Harrow cricket match was the equivalent of the Army-Navy football game in the United States.

The family stayed with the young boy for a few days. Then they left for the continent, to visit a spa for Mrs. Nehru's health, and to look for the best motor cars that Motilal could find. For the first time in his life, Jawaharlal was left alone, away from his family and country.

Was he homesick? He was, of course. True, the Harrovians were friendly, but this was an alien world just the same. There was another young Indian at school, a highborn young man called Paramjit Sungh, son of the Maharaja of Kapurthala, but he was no companion. An arrogant, foppish youngster, he was universally disliked. It did not help him in the least when he told his English classmates that if they were to set foot in his ancestral land he would revenge himself for their superior attitude toward him.

How did young Jawaharlal fare in this upper-class British school? Reviewing his Harrow days in later years, he conceded that he had not been a "perfect fit," and for good reasons, too. His background was different and he, the lonely boy from the Abode of Bliss, was not used to the company of young people his own age. Also, he was conscious of living in the midst of plenty in Harrow, while people were starving in Allahabad. Many people could have lived on the food that went into Harrow's garbage cans.

Eventually, Jawaharlal did adjust himself to the English school, and he was good in most subjects. The housemaster's comment on his performance was, "Very creditable stand."

He was praised for having written some superior history papers, and he impressed his teachers with his maturity, especially in politics. At the time, a new English government came into office, prompting an instructor to ask the boys to name its members. Only the boy from India could do it.

While his classmates talked about sports, girls, visits to London, and trivialities, Jawaharlal sought conversation about politics. The Labour party was forging ahead, and Jawaharlal sympathized with its aims. He would have liked to converse about books and the theater, too, but found little response. He kept his father posted about his life at Harrow, and this correspondence served as his "lightning conductor" against nostalgia. He was often critical of his classmates, who were "more interested in their class standing than in knowledge." He failed to find most of the boys intellectually alert. Yet, some of them became England's leaders.

In a notable letter in March, 1906, Motilal wrote to his son: "I can appreciate your inability to enter into the spirit of Harrow life. An Indian boy generally is more thoughtful than an English boy of the same age. In fact, there is an early development in India which Englishmen call precocity. Whatever it is, my experience tells me that what we gain at the beginning, we lose at the end. You must have seen many English boys even older than you are, looking perfectly bland and stupid, but have you seen any Indian of the same age as Dr. Wood looking half so vivacious and full of life? This is, no doubt, due to our climate, but there it is. Childhood in England occupies a much greater portion of life than it does in India, and so do boyhood and manhood. Old age does not properly begin till a man is three score and odd—an age very seldom reached in India. Big boys in England, therefore, are to be found committing themselves to foolish pranks which much smaller boys in India would be ashamed of. But this is no reason why they should be despised. They afford you, who can think, an excellent opportunity to study at least one phase of human nature, and thus add to your particular branch of knowledge, called experience."

At Harrow, Jawaharlal Nehru received numerous prizes, mainly books. One of these made a lasting impression on him: a biography of Giuseppe Garibaldi, a main architect of Italian independence. The book was by the English historian G. M. Trevelyan. Jawaharlal detected great similarity between the India of his days and the Italy before unification under the spirited leadership of Garibaldi. Both countries had been cradles of creative civilizations. The monumental achievements of the Romans were matched by those of great Indian rulers, such as Asoka. Jawaharlal noticed similarities even in the two countries' locations; both of them southern peninsulas on a continent, both with natural frontiers—the Alps and the seas for Italy; the Himalayas, Karakorum, Hindu Kush regions, and the seas for India.

Now that the boy from Allahabad had found one hero, he went in search of others. He discovered them in George Washington, struggling for American independence against Britain; in Simon Bolivar, fighting Spain; and in Lajos Kossuth, the Hungarian, who led his country's resistance to the Hapsburg dynasty.

In Britain, young Jawaharlal had free access to books that he could not obtain in India. These books described the British people's struggle against their royal oppressors. He noticed that while the British were proud of their fight against tyranny at home, they themselves practiced despotism in their dependencies abroad. Thus, they exhibited a double personality: democratic at home, autocratic in their colonies. And why so? Because at home they had fought for their freedom, while overseas they faced people unready to make the sacrifices that they themselves had made for their democracy. India would be able to gain its freedom only by following Britain's example at home.

One of the Harrow maxims was *Mens sana in corpore sano*, "a sound mind in a sound body." Therefore, sports received close attention at school. Teamwork in sports stimulated cooperation and boosted character-forming competitive spirit. Jawaharlal joined other boys in playing cricket, frequented the school gymnasium, and joined the rifle club and the cadet corps. As the months grew into years, Jawaharlal became increasingly like an English youth. He would have been even more so had not an unidentified "magnetic force" kept attracting him to India. He was in constant correspondence with his family, and read the homeland papers. English was the language in which he best expressed himself; writing, thinking, and even dreaming in it. He acquired the clipped accents of the English higher classes. With his thinking in English came also a closer adaptation to British mentality. But he did not become completely English. Where was he more at home? He no longer knew the answer. Perhaps he belonged to both the East and West—and the world was his real home.

The years passed, and the end of his stay at Harrow approached. His class standing continued to be above average, constantly improving. Motilal had good reason to write: "You make me a very proud father, my son." The time of separation from Harrow came in the summer of 1907, accompanied by the usual parties and nostalgic singing of old favorites, such as "Jerry, You Duffer and Dunce," and, above all, "When Grandpapa's Grandpapa Was in the Lower, Lower First."

Jawaharlal was now approaching eighteen. He was handsome and dark-haired; his eyes were alight with a luminous sheen. His stay in Britain was no frivolous pastime. He was conscious of his responsibilities toward his family and his own future. This sense of responsibility was reflected on his thoughtful features. He wanted to justify his father's expectations.

He developed a reflective mind, very serious for his age, and he often wondered: What was his aim in life? He was not thinking of himself in a political role, especially since there was not much native politics in the India of those days. Nor did he think of going into government service. He knew that although in England he was accepted as a British subject, he would have been treated in India as a "lesser breed," in spite of his family's status. There was barely any government career open for a scion of a family of the Nehrus' standing, but he might become a vakil, making a pot of gold like his father. Yet, he was not money-minded and, besides, all he wanted was his for the asking.

Actually, Jawaharlal did not have to concern himself with that problem as yet. A Harrow graduate was welcome in any university of England, including Oxford or Cambridge. He applied for admission to the latter, and in October, 1907, word was relayed to Jawaharlal Nehru that he had been accepted by Trinity College, Cambridge.

What memories did he leave behind at Harrow? When he made his way up the political ladder in India in years to come, comments by former classmates at Harrow expressed their surprise. The shy young man at school now appeared to imperial-minded Britishers as a fire-eater. They could not reconcile their recollection of the dreamy-eyed young boy with his later role as the spellbinder of millions. One former schoolmate who had made his way to the House of Lords had this to say about Nehru, the prominent politician, in a letter to *The Times* of London: "Hindus do not believe that death is the ultimate end. They hold that living creatures continue to live after their apparent deaths in successive reincarnations. Mr. Nehru has not waited to get reincarnated. He has become an entirely different creature already during his lifetime. I do not recognize the modest boy I knew at Harrow in the political agitator I read about in the press."

More favorable was the recollection of Nehru's house-master, the Reverend Stogdon, who remembered him as a "nice boy, quiet, and refined. While he was not demonstrative, one felt great strength of character in him. I should doubt if he told many boys what his opinions were. . . ."

Jawaharlal entered Trinity College, Cambridge, in 1907. "A slim, handsome, dark-haired youth," biographer Frank Moraes describes him, "with sensitive eyes, speaking English in the consciously clipped accents of a British public school boy." For three years his home was Cambridge. He took the Natural Science Tripos, chemistry, geology, and botany. His performance was creditable but not outstanding. In his rather detached way, he was fond of Cambridge, whose historic sites deeply stirred his sense of the past. His esthetic sense attracted him to the famous cloister court of Trinity College, a "marvel of pleasing proportions," and to its historic main quadrangle, with its landmark, the early seventeenth-century fountain.

He not only talked like an Englishman, but he dressed like one, perhaps even with greater care. He was never short of money and he enjoyed himself, eating well, drinking well,

dressing well. The most expensive beverage was his favorite
—champagne. In some respects, Jawaharlal was somewhat
different from the other young men. His schoolmates called
him "the lady" because of his social reticence. He did not
seem to have girl friends.

He, who was to cast his oratorical spell on hundreds of
millions, was a shy young man at Cambridge, too. He froze
into immobility when facing an audience. Not that he did not
try to train himself for public speaking. He had joined the
college debating society, The Magpie and the Stump, but he
had hardly ever dared to get up and speak. The members who
did not participate in debates had to pay a fine, and Nehru
paid it frequently.

In due time young Nehru had to face the future—his
career. The opportunities open to a young man of his background were mainly two—the Indian Civil Service and the
law. But he did not seem to have an interest in either field.

His extracurricular activities did indicate his inclination:
reading and politics. In Cambridge he became interested in
socialism. His composed nature attracted him to a mild variety of it—Fabian socialism, so named after a military leader
of classical Rome who gained his ends not by rushing into
battles but by biding his time, relying upon the effect of his
wearying tactics on the foe. Historic developments, the
Fabians held, were gradual and could not be forced. They
were also inevitable. Some of the greatest minds of Britain
were Fabians—George Bernard Shaw, H. G. Wells, Sidney
Webb, Bertrand Russell. Young Nehru felt comfortable in
their distinguished company.

At Cambridge, there was also an Indian colony, mainly the
sons of prominent parents. They formed an organization of

their own called the Majlis. Jawaharlal joined that, too, but took no active part in it. His own countrymen considered him aloof.

Having grown to manhood in English schools, he was again torn by an inner contradiction. Did he feel more at home in Britain than in India? He was not sure and this indecision about his place in the world was to haunt him all his life. Was he of the West or of the East? Years later, he expressed his doubts vividly: "I am a stranger and alien in the West, I cannot be of it. But in my own country, also, sometimes, I have an exile's feelings."

The traditional terms of the Cambridge academic year followed one another in quick succession: Michaelmas, Lent, and Easter. The three undergraduate years were soon over, and then came the tests. First, the examination which had the quaint designation of "Little Go"—consisting of classical and modern languages, mathematics, and history or religion. Nehru did not pass them with flying colors but passed them well enough to take the second set of tests of honors degree in his specialty. He received second-class honors in natural sciences.

Then came the decision—Indian Civil Service or the law? I.C.S. had some appeal for him but he was only twenty—too young to take the qualifying test. So it had to be the law— there was no other choice.

He moved to London to study law for two years. Again he studied in a historic school, the Inner Temple, where he passed his examinations "with neither glory nor ignominy," as he put it. Now he was so used to the English way of life that he would have welcomed a continued stay. But his father reminded him that his sojourn in Britain was the means, not the aim. In the summer of 1912, Jawaharlal was admitted to the bar in London. He had been in England for over seven years, and was now ready to return home.

England was basking then in the afterglow of a golden age. Life was good for people of affluence, such as Jawaharlal, and it was increasingly better for others, too. So it was with an aching heart that Jawaharlal Nehru bade goodbye to London, drenched by rain and yet so glowingly attractive to the young Brahman, as he cast a fond look at it from the deck of the Peninsular and Oriental steamer bound for India.

∿ THREE ∿

Back to India

The Peninsular and Oriental liner listed as one of its first-class passengers, "Jawaharlal Nehru, Esq." After his long stay in England, he was on his way to Anand Bhawan, the House of Bliss in the town of Allah, Allahabad—his home. He had plenty of time to think about his life on the long voyage. Home? Was India really his home? He had been in Britain for seven years, and there his way of life and his intellectual habits were formed. His favorite writers were English, the immortals of Western literature. He not only talked but also thought in English. He loved that language,

47

the tongue of Shakespeare and Milton; he had learned to use its rich shadings, so expressive, practical, and poetical.

He saw the British flag at all important points on his way home: halfway around the globe, at Gibraltar, Malta, at Suez, at Aden, on the high seas. The ship followed the lifeline of the empire, linking the "tight little island" with its crowded vast peninsular empire. What would be his first impression in his native land?

The Gateway of India—Bombay—hove into sight, bathed in the flames of the tropical sun. The sky was a deep azure, fading into the purple horizon where the heavenly canopy touched the sea. Young Nehru had forgotten about the heat in his native land, and he was annoyed. The very sea must be boiling hot, he thought. With some nostalgia, he remembered the misty nights in London on the Thames embankment in the shadow of Westminster, looming tremendously large, a physical reality and the embodiment of history. Rain and cold in England had been his constant companions, and now he was enwrapped by blazing heat.

The immigration and customs officials at Bombay were British, speaking the language of the common people. One of them was a London cockney, the other a Midlander, dropping their *h*'s, and using the simple words of simple people. Nehru answered their clipped questions in the accents of Cambridge and Harrow. The officials treated him with the disdain that men in authority displayed in those days. His superior use of English struck them as affectation, and they detained him longer than they did the other passengers. This was his reintroduction to his native land.

Motilal was waiting, surrounded by a bevy of servants. Also waiting was his father's latest acquisition, a new shining car from Italy. It was to take them only to the railway station, because traveling to their home by rail was smoother and quicker than by auto. Motilal was as proud of his car as a child of his new toy.

While they were stowing their luggage in the car, the gangplank of the ship was surrounded by policemen wielding their *lathis,* long clubs, to protect the passengers from the pleas of the beggars. But the beggars could not be kept away. They broke through the police cordon, holding out skeletal hands for alms. The eyes of many of them were haunting— marked by the fear of rejection. Nehru fumbled in his pockets for small coins, and when he failed to find them he turned to Motilal.

"They will tear you to pieces if you give them alms," his father warned. "Beware." Quickly he thrust his son into the car and they were off. Eyes filled with despair was young Nehru's welcome to India.

"Alms are not the solution," his father admonished him.

"What is the solution?"

"You," the father replied, "and your generation. But about that some other time."

The car took them to the railway station in time for the Allahabad Mail Express. The train was tracing a long plume of smoke across the Indian heartland, the Ganges plains. It raced past hundreds of hamlets with their tens of thousands of huts, thatched-roofed with mud-brick walls. People were working in the fields, wading deep in the water of rice paddies, wielding heavy scythes on the verdant grass, and plowing furrows. At the approach of the iron monster they looked up, gazing at the train. In Britain, young Nehru had loved to stand in the corridor of the train cars, surveying the countryside, reciprocating the farmer's friendly smiles. In India, there were only sorrowful faces, as if the peasants were seeing the train as a way of escape that was closed to them. Nehru could not help thinking that the way people looked at the speeding trains reflected their national traits.

Then came the arrival at Anand Bhawan, with bustling servants all over the place showing their pleasure at the sight of the young master after so many years. Every wish of his was anticipated and every service rapidly performed. In Britain, he had learned to be his own servant. Why should an older man be the servant of a younger one? He was young and sturdy and could take care of himself. But he could not alter India's ancient ways.

Britain had provided him with the education to help him follow in his father's footsteps. Nehru was a magic name in the plains. Motilal was in high fashion among the *zamindars,* the owners of the large estates, the rich, and the absentee landowners.

These people entered horses in the Paris and Deauville races; were the best customers of expensive Savile Row London tailors. They were lavish with money and the most generous hosts. Often they had litigation about ownership rights, claims against the government of India or their own people. They could afford the best legal service, and Motilal Nehru had the reputation of being the best. But he had time to take only so many cases, and the rich people competed for his services. Young Nehru, with his education in Britain's elite schools, could now help out his father. But he impressed the older man as being uninterested in money. Yet, Motilal knew that people did not appreciate an attorney unless his charges were high.

Twenty-three years of age now, young Nehru was expected to leap from the warm obscurity of his paternal home into the chilling stream of everyday life. Having prepared himself for a career in law, he was expected to enter into partnership with his father. Motilal was a sturdy man in his fifties and retirement was not in his mind, but he might get tired after another decade or two of intensive work and his son was to be the heir of his lush practice. There was much talk about legal problems in the House of Bliss, and in 1912, Jawaharlal was admitted to the Allahabad bar.

The legal system in India was then a veritable rabbit warren, with a maze of twists and turns. It had grown up on several levels, corresponding to the changing fortunes of the peninsula, as new masters emerged. Deposited in the course of centuries and responding to the needs of a society in which castes predetermined every person's niche, the legal system contained many layers of law. Superimposed upon the old traditional law was the more recent heritage of the Muslim conquerors, introducing new principles imported from alien ways. The British rule deposited still another legal system, and more complications were posed by the customs of hundreds of princely states.

"What could be more exciting than this law system of countless hues?" Motilal exhorted his son. "No two cases are similar even in their smallest details. In our laws there is not one dull word."

"But does this variety make sense?" his son asked. "After all, there can be only one truth, and not a choice of them. And how do you find truth in a maze of contradictions?"

"Well, my son," Motilal answered, "you'll learn. Law—as nearly everything else—is common sense applied to everyday life."

Following his father's advice, young Nehru went dutifully to the lawcourts. But he failed to find the excitement that Motilal found. Perhaps the fledgling lawyer was annoyed by the fact that Britishers were the judges. He was, in fact, sickened by the attitude of many clients at court. They were rich people and tyrants at home, but in court they were obsequious, never forgetting to scatter the words, "May it please your Lordships," and in all their depositions fawning even upon the British clerks, whom they considered a superior breed.

Young Nehru was alienated by other factors in the law practice, too. He took only cases that appeared to have truth on their side. But he found that more often than not the white color of truth was mixed with the gray of doubt. He was expected to remove these gray spots when presenting the case to court, and then he felt that his hands were not clean, especially in instances where deviations from the truth came to light only at the trial.

Soon young Nehru was forced to make a depressing discovery. His heart was not in the practice of law. Motilal's keen eyes also detected his son's doubts about his career. While Motilal himself had a mission in the courts, his son pursued only a profession. Was young Nehru attracted to another career?

Yes, he was—to politics. In Britain, he had learned that it was a citizen's duty to participate in the democratic process. That meant even to criticize the authorities. But in India, one was not expected to criticize, because the government was supposed to be without blemish or flaw. An Englishman by education, an Indian by birth, he was in an awkward position. What was he to do?

The split nature of his existence hurt him, and that is why he wore a doleful expression, mirroring a sadness in contrast to his father's roaring exuberance. Motilal was so wrapped up in his work and social life that he failed to notice the real

India which his son discovered. He also failed to see why his son was depressed. He only resented it, and so there were frictions—father roaring at son, and son reacting with impatient rejoinders. It all stemmed from the fact that Motilal thought that all was well with his world in the Abode of Bliss, while his son held that life could not be lived in installments, and that his neighbor's degradation entailed his own humiliation. In a word—father and son, endowed with different temperaments, did not get along well.

Young Nehru was constantly torn by doubts. Law did not attract him, and politics did not appear to be truthful. The occupations open to Brahmans were limited. He could have become an official in the British service but there he would have had to restrain his public-spirited instincts. "What's good for Britain is good for India" was the guideline of the British administration. Young Nehru would not be allowed to tell his British superior officers that in certain instances Britain's ambrosia was poison for India.

The British seemed to be so firmly entrenched in India that there appeared to be no possibility of getting them out. Both geography and history proved that India was England's pivot. For generations now the British had erected a global bulwark for the protection of their most precious possession, seeing to it that no hostile force appeared within a broad perimeter. They staked out claims across the oceans to keep competitors out of sight. Should they lose India—which was inconceivable—their frail little island would become the target of aggressive powers. They had to hold on to the subcontinent at all cost.

About that time, Nehru heard of a strange little man across the seas, Mohandas Karamchand Gandhi, who had made a name for himself in South Africa. A large colony of

East Indians lived there. South African whites of Dutch descent, and British settlers, fearing submergence in a sea of color, were determined to reduce the non-Europeans, including Gandhi's countrymen, to a low civic status. The Indians were a small minority, composed of traders and farm workers. If their status was lowered, they would be at the mercy of the aggressive whites. Mohandas Gandhi had been asked to fight for the Indians' cause.

He organized them against this policy of discrimination, and gave them a weapon more powerful than arms. Its name was *satyagraha* (sut-yuh-*gruh*-huh), conquering by truth. The fight against injustice was to be nonviolent. The victims of this fight pledged not to cooperate with the authorities in the latter's design to commit injustice. Mass demonstrations were to awaken the public conscience of fair-minded people. Such demonstrations were forbidden by the authorities, and by leading them, Gandhi courted jail. Many times he was imprisoned, and eventually his cell became a podium from which his voice was heard all over South Africa, then in India, and, finally, throughout the world. His weapon served the cause of people who were strong in their sense of justice, but weak in physical force.

Newspapers in India began to take notice of "the little brown man," and his features became familiar on the peninsula. He looked like a wise owl, a human owl with iron-framed spectacles perched on the saddle of his sloping nose. It was through the papers that Nehru first heard about Gandhi.

One day late in 1914, there was a big commotion among Indians interested in public affairs. A boat had arrived from overseas and down the gangplank came the frail little man with the owlish face, welcomed by a huge throng. Gandhi had returned to his native land. Soon he was in the van of a satyagraha movement against British rule in India.

"And then came Gandhi," Nehru was to say some years later. "He was like a powerful current of fresh air that made us stretch ourselves and take deep breaths; like a beam of light that pierced the darkness and removed the scales from our eyes; like a whirlwind that upset many things, but most of all the working of people's minds. He did not descend from the top; he seemed to emerge from the millions of India, speaking their language and incessantly drawing attention to them and their appalling condition." This is how Jawaharlal Nehru found his mission in the life of India.

Before Gandhi's arrival, a shot had been fired in a little-known street in the center of a little-known town. That shot played a role in the lives of both Nehru and Gandhi. The town was in the heart of the Balkan peninsula in southeastern Europe. Soon its name became known throughout the world —Sarajevo. The shot had killed Archduke Francis Ferdinand, heir to the throne of Austria-Hungary. It was the signal for the outbreak of World War I, as history was to know it. In that war most major countries were involved, with Great Britain in the van.

Young Nehru paid some attention to the shot, but not too much. Europe had had many wars in the past, and so he thought, at first, what if another one has been added to the list? It seemed a foolish war to him and besides he felt that all wars were foolish. Because an unpleasant Austrian archduke had been killed in a Balkan town, probably thousands of people would be killed in turn. Nehru could not know at the time that not thousands but millions would be killed in the war. He could not know—nor could others—that this was to become an important event in India's history, too.

In the war, Britain found itself in a deadly struggle with its chief enemies, headed by Germany. But Britain's trouble could be India's opportunity. This link between events in the West and India was seen clearly by some observers, one of whom was the astute English woman, Annie Besant, now approaching old age and yet still filled with irrepressible energy. As leader of the Theosophical Society, she held that the Hindus' contemplative life was especially helpful in reaching moments of illumination when one was filled with the "presence of God." In Benares, the holiest of all Indian cities, she set up the Central Hindu College, in which the sacred writings of India formed the core of the curriculum and in which India's special mission in the world was taught. Mrs. Besant's thoughts appealed to the Nehrus.

Annie Besant founded the India Home Rule League, which claimed self-government for the Indians on humanitarian and religious grounds. The British had no right, this English woman said, to claim that they represented a higher level of culture: the Hindus possessed spiritual superiority. In view of that, and because Britain needed to keep India quiet and to concentrate on winning the war, India, said Mrs. Besant, should be given self-government, or home rule. She argued that even though the Indian people ought to remain linked with Britain in foreign affairs, diplomacy, and defense, they should be free to arrange their domestic affairs according to their own best interests. The British arrested Mrs. Besant.

The war went on. The two opposing camps—the Entente, consisting of Russia, Britain, and France, and the Central Powers, headed by Germany—were of about equal strength, and the struggle remained in a stalemate for three years. Then in 1917, the United States moved in to aid the Entente, and that decided the outcome. The Central Powers lost. Troops from India had helped to win the war. Annie Besant had been freed, and the Nehrus now expected the British to pursue a more liberal policy.

"Make the world safe for democracy," Woodrow Wilson, President of the United States, had declared. Many Indians thought that this voice was the conscience of a new phase of man's history. The America that had spoken was associated with Britain, which ruled over India. India's population of three hundred million was the largest of any part of the British Empire. Was democracy to be extended to the subcontinent? Annie Besant said yes. Gandhi said yes. And the Nehrus said yes. All were impatient to be shown British intentions.

Britain passed a Government of India Act. Did it give India more freedom to decide its own fate? It did nothing of the kind. Power continued to rest mainly in the hands of the British, the secretary of state for India, and the viceroy. The reforms were very timid and provided that the legislative council of the viceroy, which was merely an advisory body, should be accessible to Indians. Limited powers in the provinces of India were transferred to officials elected by a small part of the population.

"It is a fraud," Motilal Nehru roared. He had moved closer to his son's view that India was ready for a great change. Annie Besant agreed that the act was a deception. Gandhi, the man of peace, also rejected the limited reform. He now took matters in hand and gradually became the conscience of India.

The Indian National Congress was the expression of Indian nationalism, and from its platform Gandhi addressed his people. Until now the Congress had been a polite discussion group mainly of the well-bred, well-dressed, and well-heeled castes. Members of the higher social classes found there a meeting place to exchange views that seldom went beyond mild criticism of the British.

But with Gandhi, the complexion of the Congress party changed. Its color had been white—white-collar. Now it was transformed into dun, the color of the garments of the peasants and industrial workers, of India's millions. At first, the white-collar members were dismayed, but gradually they rallied to Gandhi's views. Peasants and workers, normally awed by the superior airs of the white-collar crowd, slowly gained self-confidence and began to voice their views on their problems. Thus the Congress became a popular party, much to the delight of Nehru, the intellectual aristocrat. He held that without mass support India could never see a new dawn.

Not all of Gandhi's followers understood his views. Some of them said that violence was the only language the British understood. Gandhi countered this view with a new weapon of nonviolence, the *hartal,* the complete cessation of public activities to the point where public life was immobilized. No recourse to the courts, no classes for the children, no payment of taxes, no use of public transportation. Such a hartal was to be carried out peacefully. But peaceful plans were one thing; the way they were carried out was another. Riots could be caused by trigger-happy army officers or knife-happy countrymen. Trouble from the former broke out in the city of Amritsar.

In the wake of World War I and all its expectations, revolts kept flaring up in India. Quickly, the British parliament passed the so-called Rowlatt Acts early in 1919, giving the government special powers to deal with its Indian subjects, including imprisonment without trial. This was followed by an incident at the Golden Temple of Amritsar, and then by a massacre.

Amritsar, in the northwest, is the sacred city of the important religious sect, the Sikhs. It derives its name from its Pool of Immortality—*Amrita Saras*—cradling a small island containing the Golden Temple with one large and several small copper domes sheathed with gilded foil. The gilded walls, the roof, the cupolas with vivid touches of red, are mirrored in the pool—a pleasant sight.

However, on an April day in 1919, some Sikhs decided that a couple of British ladies, who were out walking, had showed a disrespectful attitude toward the shrine. The Sikhs made some insulting remarks and the ladies presented their complaints to the authorities.

The commanding officer of the armed forces in the province of Punjab was General Reginald Harry Dyer, a martinet. Promptly, he issued directives that when Indians came to the spot where the ladies had been allegedly insulted, they must get down on all fours. He appeared to believe that order could be best maintained by keeping the "natives" in their places.

This British insult, combined with the Rowlatt Acts, aroused the townspeople, who had called a mass meeting of protest in defiance of the authorities. The demonstrators were Sikhs, as well as Muslims and Hindus. Their meeting place was a public garden, Jallianwala Bagh, fenced in by walls and houses. The garden had only one very narrow exit lane. When thousands of protesters were assembled, Dyer marched his soldiers into this enclosure. Without giving the people a chance to take cover or disperse, he ordered his soldiers to fire at them. A frantic stampede followed. Since the narrow exit path was crowded, people tried to save their lives by climbing across the wall. Dyer gave a command to his soldiers to direct their fire at them. The carnage was so great that soon the soil of the meeting place was soaked with blood. Hundreds of people died, the lowest estimate being four hundred.

Diehard members of the British community hailed Dyer as the savior of the Punjab, and presented him with a sword of honor. To Indians, April 13, 1919, the date of the massacre, became a day of shame.

Shortly after this bloody event, Jawaharlal Nehru happened to take the night train from Amritsar to Delhi, traveling in an upper berth. Unobserved, he overheard the conversation of a group of British officers in the lower berths. One of them gave a detailed and boastful account of the massacre. He was General Dyer.

The Amritsar Massacre became a milestone in Indian history. Gandhi, a man of moderation, could no longer restrain himself, and he denounced the British rule in India as "diabolic," the harshest term he ever used. He realized that now he had to deal not only with reasonable Englishmen but also with bigots who were more considerate of the life of a dog than of an Indian.

Jawaharlal Nehru, too, felt impelled to alter his moderate views. "Moderation," he remarked, "fails when dealing with immoderate people." Then he added, "Murder does not become patriotism when other 'breeds' are involved."

The Amritsar Massacre effected a change on another citizen of Allahabad. Motilal, at the outset of his career uncritical of British rule and later moderately critical, now joined hands with his son in denouncing official terrorism. It had been in his interest not to rock the boat, and to accept the inevitability of British rule, but now he effected a turn-about, throwing in his lot with the Congress party, even though some of his fellow barristers might disagree and British judges might frown on his act. He also ran the danger of having some of his princely clients and rich landowners leave him for "less controversial" barristers. But he no longer cared. Now for the first time he saw that both Gandhi and his son were right in opposing British rule. His own pro-British attitude had fallen with the victims of Amritsar.

～ FOUR ～

A Wedding and the Jail

Her name was Kamala—lotus flower—and she was seventeen. There was a flowerlike delicacy about her, a physical frailty. Her large questing eyes lighted up a finely chiseled, oval face; her skin was taut and smooth. She was slim, and a little above average height. Of education she had next to nothing—a little schooling at home. He had the best education the Western world could offer, and he was twenty-seven. The marriage took place in March, 1916. The average life expectation in India in those days was thirty. In this setting, Jawaharlal Nehru was not a young man when he got married.

His wife was also of Brahman caste from the mountainous

world of Kashmir, and Kaul was her family name, too. The
marriage was arranged by the parents of the bride and groom,
as was customary in India. Although Jawaharlal was not a
tradition-minded person, tradition was followed in the
selection of his spouse and in his wedding. Tradition was
not followed, on the other hand, in his getting married so
late.

In India at that time, child marriages were very common.
A succession of offspring was essential to perform the religious rites after the father's death. People died young, so
they had to get married young. One-fifth of India's children
were wedded by the age of ten. Most of the marriages—about
70 per cent—took place between the ages of ten and fifteen.

But in households like the Nehrus' there was no urgent
need for an early marriage. Jawaharlal was not concerned
with religious rites after his death. Yet traditions had to be
observed even among the moderns. An auspicious day had to
be chosen for the wedding, to please the gods. It took place
on the festival day of Vasanta Panchami, dedicated to the
goddess Sarasvati, the consort of Brahma. The goddess was
patroness of arts, sciences, learning, and speech. The month,
March, had a special appeal to the Kashmiri, for it is in the
early spring when nature's budding forces begin their climb
up the slopes of the sky-scraping mountain abodes of the
gods. The year 1916 was one of comparative peace in India,
while much of the rest of the world was uneasy with the
threat of war. At the wedding ceremony, the bride in a pink
sari and the groom on a white steed made a dashing couple.

Was it a good marriage? Nehru was still trying to find
himself, still unsure of what field to choose. Addicted to
brooding, he continued to be the Allahabad Hamlet, ready

for great deeds, but frustrated by India's plight and not
knowing where to begin. Because of his moods and frustra-
tions, he did not have much time for his fragile wife. He did
not know that Kamala, even though poorly educated, was
also interested in India's plight and would have liked to be
drawn into his confidence. He was to learn only later that the
fragile lotus flower had strong fibers. She was a young woman
of character, and able to make decisions. Much, much later
he was to learn that she was ready to sacrifice even her freedom for the common people's cause. It was much later, too,
that Nehru was able to analyze his own weaknesses as a
husband. "I was a most unsatisfactory person to marry," he
said.

And so a year passed, a historic year on the battlefields as
the United States joined the Allies and paved the way for
victory, and Gandhi waged a campaign of satyagraha. But
the great news in the Nehrus' Abode of Bliss was the birth,
on November 19, 1917, of a daughter named Indira—moon.
She was a particularly attractive child, and so the parents
also named her Priyadarshini, "pleasant to behold." Who
could have foretold that the baby girl was to grow into a
historic personality, one whose very presence was a blessing?

Physically fragile, Kamala suffered from a condition, the
true nature of which had not been diagnosed. If miracle drugs
had been in use in those days, they could have been of help
in the Nehru household. But Kamala was weak, and her
child had to be left to the servants most of the time. Years
later it was learned that Kamala was afflicted with tuberculosis.

Having met Gandhi at the Lucknow meeting of the Congress party in 1916, Jawaharlal fell under the spell of the
"little brown man." It was not the spell that the orator or the

charlatan casts on his audience. It was the spell of a man of truth.

"Gandhi was always there as a symbol of uncompromising truth to pull us up and shame us into truth. . . . Different persons may and do take different views of truth, and each individual is powerfully influenced by his own background, training and impulses. So also Gandhi. But truth is at least for an individual what he himself feels and knows to be true. According to this definition I do not know of any person who holds to the truth as Gandhi does. This is a dangerous quality in a politician, for he speaks out his mind and even lets the public see its changing phases."

It was the pursuit of this truth in the presence of Gandhi that kept Jawaharlal away from home much of the time. Nehru became Gandhi's *chela,* a disciple, and then a *guru,* a teacher, trying to carry the truth to the people.

Kamala stayed at home, attending to the child as much as she could. She also educated herself, not to the level of her husband but closer to him, by studying English, which was spoken in the household more than Hindi.

Indira saw little of her parents. Her father was away much of the time and her mother was now beginning to show the telltale symptom of her ailment—fever.

Was Nehru's oldest sister to be a mother-substitute to the child? The age difference between the two was seventeen years. There was a radiance about this aunt, who was a real beauty and the best-looking member of an attractive family. There was an aura about her, too—this young woman with the figure of a goddess, scintillating eyes, quick smile, and tempestuous frowns. What made her particularly attractive was her intelligence, reflected in her entire bearing. Like the other Nehrus, she was strong-willed; and like her father,

Motilal, she could be a human tornado, explosive in mirth and wrath.

She was self-centered, too—another Nehru trait. The beautiful young woman began to be caught up in India's accelerating whirlwind of politics and began to throw herself into freedom movements. She continued her education, kept abreast of the world by reading books, and—naturally—had rounds of social obligations. She could not devote much time to her niece.

If it had not been for Grandpa Motilal, the Abode of Bliss might not have been too blissful for the little child. Not that Motilal had more time than the younger members of the household. Now he himself was deeply involved in politics and he was still the top-ranking barrister at the Allahabad court. Nor was he less strong-willed than his brood. But he always managed to spare time for his grand-child. To him, Indira was not only the most beautiful creature in the world but the most miraculous product of creation—so bright and perceptive, a "miniature miracle." And how she liked to play with Grandpa! The most dignified star of the Allahabad bar was her best "mount," as he got on all fours for the mirthful grandchild to get upon his back. Apart from these happy hours with her grandfather, life was lonely for the little girl in the grand house, as it had been lonely for her father.

Meanwhile, a momentous change occurred in the world. At long last, the war was over, and mankind was yearning for peace. The people of India wanted peace, too, but not the peace of oppression. "Awakening" was the word to describe the more articulate people of the vast land. The masses now followed Gandhi, who believed in the force of truth, not the force of arms. He called upon his people to strive for *swadeshi,* reinforced by using homemade products and boycotting foreign goods. He summoned them to turn to India's traditional spinning wheel to produce *khadi,* homespun cloth. Indians did not need foreign garments. For men it was enough to wear the *dhoti* in the Indian climate, the loincloth tucked in at the waist. Women would wear their saris. Thus they would prepare the way for swadeshi, and, eventually, independence. The theme Gandhi never tired of stressing to his audiences was this: the British would benefit far more by giving up India than by holding on to her; by surrendering their hold they would gain a friendly trading partner.

In May, 1920, Nehru was back from his political wanderings. The Abode of Bliss now looked more like a hospital. His mother was ill, and there was no longer any doubt about Kamala's ailment. It was diagnosed by a number of physicians as tuberculosis. But perhaps there was still time to help. The heat of Allahabad was stifling—May is one of the toughest months in that region of the world. It was thought that the mountain air might help the two women of the Nehru household, the aging mother and the wife. It was decided, therefore, to go to the famed hill station of Mussoorie, patronized by British officials and rich Indians. Standing on a ridge more than six thousand feet up in the lower Himalayan range, the town looks at the snow-shrouded mountain peaks. Coming from the plains into the elegance of the resort, Jawaharlal could not hide his feeling of going home to a period of his previous reincarnation—the Western way of life. He was elated by the mountain air but saddened by his rediscovery of the duality within himself. He realized that he liked the distinguished setting.

An aristocratic hostelry, the Savoy, became the temporary

family residence. Again, Nehru was more preoccupied with himself than with his family. He liked to take long solitary walks, enjoying the crystal-clear air, reading, meditating, and daydreaming.

A short time before the arrival of the family, there had been a boundary clash on India's mountainous border with neighboring Afghanistan, and it was to affect the family's stay in the resort. With a view to settling the border incident, British and Afghan representatives met at the Savoy. So engrossed was Nehru in his thoughts that he was not even aware of the diplomatic parley. But events were to show that the British were aware of his presence in the hill town.

The family was sitting at breakfast one morning, marveling at the breathtaking mountain scenery, when there was a knock on the door and in stomped a Gurkha mountaineer, the orderly of a high British officer in charge of town security. After saluting the family smartly, the orderly handed a document to Nehru, containing an official externment order, which required him to leave the district within twenty-four hours. No appeal was possible.

From this incident, Nehru learned a lesson. The authorities were distrustful of him and suspected him of being in town with political motives in mind. He learned, too, that he was very well known to the authorities, who kept their eyes on him. The suspicion of political motives in this instance was unjustified, and Nehru felt aggrieved. He returned to Allahabad a wiser man. Now he knew from first-hand experience that he had to watch his step.

After the incident, he moved closer to the people who were even more exposed to arbitrary actions than he. These were *kisans,* or peasants. They had been told that in Allahabad there was a wise man by the name of Gandhi who could help them. So they came to see the man whom his countrymen were to call Mahatma, the Great Soul. The peasants learned that they had been misinformed, and that Gandhi was hundreds of miles away. But there was Nehru, a leading Gandhi disciple. They approached him with their woes.

There were two hundred kisans now in the neighborhood of Allahabad, at the point where the Jumna and the Ganges rivers meet at the *prayag,* the place of pilgrimage where devout Hindus came by the thousands to wash off their sins. Nehru found them in a ravine near the stream, and they told their woes to him. Typical was the case history of Narayan, a kisan from the village of Satna.

Narayan worked for a taluqdar (ta-*luk*-dar), a landowner, who made his life bitter. This poor peasant had no land of his own; he was a sharecropper. For two days a week he had to perform household chores for the taluqdar, for whom he also had to work on the land. The food he produced on his share of the land was so little that he had to retain a small portion of the produce that was due to the taluqdar. When this was discovered, Narayan received an order to appear at the taluqdar's house, and there he was flogged till blood covered his body. Like other ill-treated farmers, he did not dare complain to the authorities. Narayan and his fellow kisans had hoped that Gandhi could help them, but now that they had failed to find him they were afraid to return to their hamlets because their masters were going to have them beaten mercilessly for leaving.

Nehru listened to their stories and asked questions. How large a family did Narayan have? Six of his children were alive; four had died. How old was he? He did not know. Nehru guessed that he must have married before the age of fourteen, and that the Narayans had their children in quick

succession. Although he could not have been more than
thirty, he looked like an old man, with countless wrinkles
on his cheeks and stumps of blackened teeth in his mouth.

Nehru's sympathy heartened the peasants, who now im-
plored him to accompany them to Satna. He agreed to their
request, and was shattered by the sight. He had seen many
villages all over India—poverty-stricken places where famine
stared him in the face. Yet until then, he had never stayed
in a kisan hut. This time he spent a night there. With the
dusk it was plunged into darkness, for the peasants could
not afford a candle. The hut was filled with an acrid smell,
which did not come from smoke because the dwellers had no
food to cook. It was the smell of rotting straw on the thatched
roof, decomposed by the myriads of insects flourishing in the
heat and the monsoon.

White-gray specters appeared in the dark—three generations of the family. The whites of their eyes seemed abnor-
mally large in small faces. Their skin was stretched tautly over
bony frames. Nehru saw the eyes of listless babies so hungry
that they had lost the strength to cry, the lusterless eyes of
parents no longer sustained by hope, and the eyes of a grandmother, a toothless hag with grayish wispy hair. How old was
this ancient woman? Very, very old, he was told. He insisted:
How many years? Years meant nothing to the hut dwellers.
How many monsoons? Nobody knew. She was too old; she
had been there throughout the ages. From other oldsters
Nehru finally learned that the "ancient" woman may have
been all of forty.

The villagers gave him more details about the exactions
and cruelties of the taluqdar. His sheriffs beat the children
mercilessly if their weakness kept them from performing
their endless chores. And what did the authorities do about

this? Nehru asked. The authorities? The kisans were incredu-
lous. What did the word mean? The taluqdar was the only
man with power. Was he a native of the land? Yes, a man
speaking their language, but even though he spoke the same
tongue, there was no link between him and the peasants.
Neighbors in space, they were worlds apart in fact. Nehru
asked the peasants what he could do for them? He could
do what he was doing in their village, the peasants told
him—visiting them in the huts and letting the invisible
radiance of godlike persons fall upon them.

Nehru was invited to spend another night in the hut, but
he could not go through the experiences of the previous night
again. He spent the second night in the open, where the air
was scented by the camphor bush. These were sleepless hours
in which his thinking underwent a great change. He had been
interested in the condition of the peasants before this night,
and he had wanted less of the British influence and more
of the Indian in his country. But until that night, words like
self-government had represented merely an abstract thought
to him. Now he learned that such thoughts acquired real
meaning if related to peasants such as Narayan, his famished
family, and to the taluqdar. Henceforth, freedom meant to
Nehru not only the right of the people to trudge to polling
booths and to select their delegates to the Congress party.
It meant their right to rearrange their affairs in such a way
that Narayan would be able to feed his family and send his
children to school to acquire skills that would enable them to
make their way in the world. Then, perhaps they would not
have to die before they reached thirty.

Three days and three nights later, Nehru left the village in
darkness. But he had seen the light.

Soon word spread in the neighborhood that the visitor's

name was not Nehru, but Krishna, their favorite god. Now the peasants felt less unhappy because having looked upon the god's countenance they felt twice blessed. And if some of them were to die within a monsoon period, the darshan would escort them into their new reincarnation. They hoped that after Nehru's visit, *samsara,* the transmigration of the soul, would assure them a higher status in their next life.

Musing upon his introduction to the Indian village, Nehru summed up his impressions in these words: "Looking at the peasants, their misery and overflowing gratitude, I was filled with shame and sorrow—shame at my own easy-going and comfortable life and our petty politics of the city which ignored this vast multitude of semi-naked sons and daughters of India, sorrow at their degradation and overwhelming poverty. A new picture of India seemed to rise before me, naked, starving, crushed, and utterly miserable. And the peasants' faith in us, casual visitors from the distant city, embarrassed me, and filled me with a new responsibility that frightened me."

After his stay in the village, Nehru was besought by country folk to visit them so that they might look upon a countenance from which the divine radiance emanated. The number of people making their pilgrimages to him constantly increased. They spoke alien tongues, so that most of them did not follow his words. But the words were unimportant; important was the radiance. To many peasants his doleful look was an asset, indicating that he was in communion with the Hindus' forty crores of gods.

When speaking to the peasants, Nehru did not always follow in Gandhi's footsteps. While he agreed with Gandhi's doctrine of nonviolence, he did not agree with the master's view that India must return to the primitive ancestral tools. He had

to agree, of course, that factories belched dirty smoke, but they
also produced more goods and paid higher wages than the
primitive jenny. Nor was Nehru religious in Gandhi's sense
of the word. Nehru did not believe in the Hindu gods. His
own creed was tailored to his needs. His was an ethical
religion—bearing in mind that every one of his deeds and
words should serve as guide to others. He also believed
that his fellowman's welfare was everybody's concern.

"Call me a do-gooder, if you like," he would say. "Should
I be a do-badder? What is wrong with trying to aid my
fellow-wanderers in India's sorrowful vale? Bear this in
mind—helping others you prepare better conditions for your
own welfare. The better off your fellow man is, the more
you prosper." Although constantly concerned with others,
basically he was a loner. But he realized that in politics one
had to act in unison. The Congress party was far from
perfect, but it provided a framework for action, even though
it contained too many time-servers trying to exploit the
public need for their own advantage, for fame and fortune.
Nehru had no choice but to work within the Congress party.
He was active in its Allahabad office, so absorbed in work
that he often stayed there until very late.

One night an event occurred involving a Prince Charming
and the authorities. The Prince Charming was the son of
the king of England, George V, whose full title was King of
the United Kingdom of Great Britain and Ireland, of the
Britannic territories beyond the seas, defender of the faith,
Emperor of India. The king's son was Edward (later the
Duke of Windsor), a dashing young man, and unmarried as
yet.

It was said that while ardent Muslims turned toward Mecca
in their prayers, hopeful unmarried princesses turned in their

prayers toward London, the home of the prince. Since the
king was the Emperor of India, too, it seemed proper to
the British government to send his representative to rally
national sentiment to the crown and to weaken the Indian
nationalist agitation. And so Prince Charming was to under-
take the trip on behalf of his royal father. Millions were to
see the young man radiating his imperial blessing.

He arrived at Bombay at the end of 1921. Darshana seemed
to be the last thing in the world that the people of India
wanted from an English prince. The streets were deserted
even in Calcutta, where thoroughfares are normally jammed.
Now even the beggars scurried out of sight. In other spots
flash riots erupted against the royal visitor, and blood marked
the imperial route. Nehru was an organizer of hartal, cessation of all work. The British authorities were incensed, as
the anticipated joyful visit turned into a sullen boycott. In
their anger, the plug-uglies of the authorities, the strong-arm
police, swung into action. Nehru was in the Allahabad
headquarters of the National Congress when he noticed that
it was being surrounded by the police, a list of names in
their hands. They called the names, and lined up the men
behind a paddy wagon. Many of Nehru's fellow workers were
picked up, but Nehru himself was left alone.

Not for long though. A few days later, on December 6,
the police surrounded the Abode of Bliss, then searched it
thoroughly. This time the police had warrants for the
arrest of father and son. The two men did not have to wait
long for the trial. It took place the following day. Motilal
was charged with being a member of the Congress Volunteers,
which the government had banned. Jawaharlal was tried on
the charge of distributing notices for the cessation of work.
Under the law this was not a criminal offense, but who

cared? One of the witnesses against Motilal offered his own application for membership in the Volunteers as evidence of guilt. This witness was a half-starved individual who evidently could not read or write, and the application he pretended to read was upside down. He perjured himself for a meal, and his testimony was accepted as proof. In the trial of Jawaharlal there was no need for a witness to perjure himself since the accused offered no defense at all. Not recognizing the jurisdiction of the court, he remained silent. The two trials took place in two different courts for two entirely different offenses, yet the sentences were identical—six months in jail.

Nehru's little girl, Indira, was present at her grandfather's trial, sitting in his arms. Her big bright eyes absorbed the unusual scene, the bewigged judges, the lawyers and guards. The strange proceedings puzzled the child, and introduced her to the courts with which members of her family, and she, too, would have close contact in years to come. Father and son were taken to the Lucknow District Jail, a hundred miles to the north. Many thousands of Congress workers were arrested and jailed, and the British administration had a problem on its hands. How to imprison so many men? This was the Nehrus' first contact, as prisoners, with jails.

All the cells were occupied when the Nehrus arrived, and so they were placed in the prison courtyard, in an unused weaving shed. There they had to make beds on the bare floor and divide the household chores. Jawaharlal got the job of cleaning the shed and doing the washing. Now the comfortable life of the Abode of Bliss, where the Nehrus were surrounded by servants, seemed to belong to another world. At home they were the masters; here they were the servants. At home there was space for privacy; in jail they were crowded into a small place with sixteen other men. Strange to say, Jawaharlal at first felt a curious elation bordering on happiness when taken to jail. Now he was one of India's suffering masses. He was lonely no more. He gave lessons in the three R's to illiterates, and in the afternoons he played volleyball. Through newspapers, which reached them regularly, the Nehrus were able to follow events outside the prison walls.

Nehru's elation was a strange phenomenon that he tried to analyze. He wanted to be part of India, and in prison he became one with his native land, in the company of the people who lived in the real world, and not in the insulated existence of the Abode of Bliss. Also, he had close contact with the varied layers of Indian life—the very poor, the middle class, and the privileged. From them, especially from the oppressed, he obtained more detailed accounts of how the people lived. Through his prison experiences Jawaharlal was better able to deepen his understanding of the ways of life of the people of his native land.

In prison, too, he had time to sort out his thoughts, to see his own place in India, and to make his future plans. In doing so, he was assailed by doubts. Would he really have the ability to get close to the people? When in the company of people with lower educational standards both he and they felt a measure of restraint. When teaching his fellow prisoners, he realized that India needed teachers who would also have to feel as one with its suffering masses and have the skills to offer remedies. He was not sure whether he was such a man. Gradually, the crowded jail got on his nerves. He wanted more privacy to give himself to his studies and thoughts.

Eventually, the six-month jail term was reduced to three, since space was in short supply. The government started a building boom—building many new jails. But before they were ready, prisoners had to be released, and that is how Nehru found himself transferred from the weaving shed of Lucknow Jail back to the comforts of the Abode of Bliss.

But the bliss was broken by a tragic event that took place early in 1922 in the little-known village of Chauri Chaura. The village is situated in the Gorakhpur District in the United Provinces, the birthplace of Gautama Buddha, the prophet of peace. It was not peace, however, which now enwrapped Chauri Chaura, but savage violence. The trouble began with a peasants' demonstration against certain policies of the authorities. They needed a permit for the demonstration, which they did not obtain. But it was held just the same, and it was unruly. The police fired on the rampaging crowd and that infuriated the peasants. Mass hysteria ensued and soon the crowd got completely out of hand. For their own protection, twenty-two constables and several local policemen sought refuge in their barracks. A madly seething crowd surrounded it and all civilized restraints were forgotten. One of the crowd, or perhaps more, set fire to the wooden barracks, which went up in flames within minutes. The policemen attempted to make a dash for their lives. The enraged peasantry prevented their escape, and the barracks became the funeral pyre of the doomed men.

When Gandhi, in the distant town of Bardoli at the time, heard about this tragedy, he was horrified. He had been telling his countrymen not to engage in acts of violence and here was their answer—the Chauri Chaura outbreak. Although this was an isolated incident, one village out of thousands, Gandhi saw the event in a different light. He saw his campaign of satyagraha totally discredited and besmirched. Acting impulsively—normally not his habit—

he called off what he and the world considered his great
contribution toward the liberation of the country. If the
struggle for a freer India, he said, degenerated into acts of
violence, he wanted no part of it. He advised his followers
to turn to a placid program of education, temperance, social
reform, and Hindu-Muslim unity. Freedom could wait.

This act of Gandhi's left the Congress party without the
unique program that offered a hope of freedom for India.
The Nehrus, among others, disapproved of the change.
They continued to exhort the people to weave their khadi
and to boycott foreign cloth, exacting pledges to that effect
from merchants. Some of the merchants broke their word and
kept on importing British goods. Thereupon Jawaharlal took
action in contravention of British law: he organized pickets
to keep customers from the offending stores. Promptly, he
was rearrested, this time on a more serious charge—criminal
intimidation and extortion. At his trial he again offered no
defense. He believed there was no use in his speaking up,
and, besides, by keeping silent he was adhering to the
principle of satyagraha, even though this would mean a
longer spell in jail. It did mean that. He was found guilty and
given a harsh sentence—a year and nine months in prison.
He was a convict now for the second time, after having spent
only six weeks as a free man.

Back at home, little Indira mounted the dining-room table
and arranged her "good" dolls. In fiery language she exhorted them to buy no British goods. Then she lined up her
"nasty" dolls, who rushed into the fray and took the demonstrators off to jail.

Jawaharlal Nehru was back in Lucknow District Jail.
This time, however, he lacked the amenities of his previous
stay because the prison authorities were better organized to

accommodate the increasing number of their involuntary guests, and they enforced a more rigid discipline. No longer were newspapers admitted into the politicals' cells, and that was a real hardship for Nehru, who could not follow events in the land. Also the number of visitors was reduced. On the other hand, Nehru now had more time to observe another world within the prison walls—that of the common criminals, murderers, bandits, burglars, and thieves. He discovered that their food rations were pitifully small. In a way, this was inevitable: the authorities did not want criminals to live better than free men. Outside the walls, countless people were starving. Were the criminals to be better off than the innocents?

Nehru was able to glean bits of information about the criminals. Some of them, he learned, seemed beyond redemption; they were the hardened types, inaccessible to attempts to reform them. Others were victims of their environment, often young people who had tried to save their kin and themselves from starvation by stealing from the rich. In fact, some of these so called criminals were gentle persons. Still others had been swept into forbidden mass actions in which they had played no active roles. They had been caught in police dragnets, thrown into prison, and thus stripped of the chance of helping their families escape starvation.

Prison life had its sunnier side, too. Books were admitted into the cells and that was a boon. At liberty, Nehru's days had been filled with administrative chores. He had barely had any time for intellectual pursuits. In jail, however, he was never engaged or in conference, and political prisoners were under no compulsion to work. He had plenty of time to read, to think, or just to dream. These were his favorite occupations. The books he liked most dealt with the intellec-

tual history of the West, especially the freedom movements
in Britain. He became absorbed in the history of his own
country, too. During his student days in England he had had
little time to become acquainted with it and now he tried to
make up for lost time. What had made his country the
cynosure of the world in the past? What was this Indian
philosophy that had exerted so great an influence on so
many profound thinkers of East and West? What were the
values that had made so many people believe in the adage,
ex oriente lux (from the East—the Light)? What was this
light that set so many great minds ablaze with admiration for
the spiritual values of his land?

Through his readings in his cell, Nehru learned much. A
graduate of Cambridge, he now became a student in what he
called his university in jail. He entered his freshman year in
Lucknow District Jail. In the course of many future stays in
prison, he was to advance from freshman to sophomore,
junior, and senior. He was to have time to enroll in post-
graduate studies, as well. In years to come he was to take
pride in his degree—P.G., prison graduate.

Nehru learned that India had given light to the world in
the teachings of the "Enlightened One"—Buddha—who
taught that life's sufferings could be best allayed by checking
ignoble desires. The great Emperor Asoka had also been
the voice of India, showing the world that peace could
score greater victories than war. Nehru's own teacher—
Gandhi—was the voice of contemporary India, fighting for
freedom by nonviolent means.

For relaxation in Lucknow Jail he turned to gardening.
There was a flower garden in the prison yard, and Nehru
became its guardian. The variety of flower colors compensated
the prisoners for the drabness of prison life. Nehru learned

that flowers—particularly roses—could be distinguished not only by their hues, but in other ways. Each of the blossoms seemed to have character traits of its own. Some of them were shy, others aggressive. The bees patronized some more than others. Some flowers went to "sleep" earlier than others; some faded more quickly. The rose became Jawaharlal's favorite flower. So strong were some of these character traits that Nehru gave names to his favorite roses—"Pertinacious," "Modest," "Aggressive." In later life he became known as the man always with a rose in his buttonhole. That was his best-known trademark.

Jail gave Nehru time not only for reading and the cultivation of flowers, but also for dreams. In the furnacelike heat of Lucknow, political prisoners were not always locked up in cells for the night, but were sometimes left to sleep in the prison yard, surrounded by walls. Nehru was one of those allowed to spend the nights under the stars. A blanket on the courtyard floor prepared him for his nocturnal spell of dreams. He liked to observe the vivid change of colors in the Indian summer sky, from deepest blue to azure and then to pink fading into purple as the sun's light struck the far horizon. Then the nocturnal sky acquired a black canopy, perforated by myriads of silvery stars. As with the rose, so with the stars. Some of them, Nehru thought, gave him a friendly wink; others appeared to be aloof. Before dozing off, he tried to fathom their mysteries. Were they worlds like the earth, and if so, did they contain human beings? If they did, were those beings as foolish as their earthly counterparts? Did they have jails for people who dared to dream of a day when all nations would be free? Or was the earth the only place where inhabitants inflicted pain on one another?

The dreams of Nehru were many-hued, like the nocturnal sky. His family appeared to him in dreams: he saw his wife and his daughter, the sunshine in his life. He often dreamed about the success of the great cause of the people of India— national freedom. He was an ambitious man, even in jail, and so the idle moments encouraged him to open the gates of the future, and he saw himself playing an important role in his land. Sometimes his dreams misted over, became clouded in fears and doubts. His father was growing old rapidly, and Jawaharlal feared for the aging man's life. Now that they had become comrades-in-arms in a fight for a happier future, Jawaharlal wondered whether Motilal was destined to see it at all.

The younger Nehru's daydreams alternated with drab reality. In prison he could not select his companions, as a free man could. As a prisoner, Nehru was compelled to see the same faces every day, month after month. Too much familiarity with his fellow inmates and their traits began to grate on his nerves. The traits became more pronounced in jail, with all its restrictions. In those cages, animal instincts spilled over. The atmosphere was poisoned, and at times, daydreams became nightmares. Nerves turned raw in prison and there was only one balm for them—liberty.

Jawaharlal Nehru was in jail on his thirty-third birthday, November 14, 1922. It was his custom on birthdays to review the past year—his accomplishments, his shortcomings. He was now "middle-aged"—indeed almost an old man by Indian standards. What could he do in the time remaining to him? The jail sentence seemed endless.

But shortly after, an amnesty was declared. On January 31, 1923, Nehru left the Lucknow District Jail.

Even though he was out of prison, he did not feel free.

because his guru Gandhi was still in jail. The soul of the Mahatma was as free as ever, but the body in which it dwelt was a captive. How could Nehru help? Could he be of use to Gandhi by assuming an important position in the provincial government? Indians did not qualify for high positions in the government, but they were allowed to hold posts in which their special knowledge counted.

After his release, Nehru was offered the post of head of the department of education in the United Provinces. He had been offered the job because he knew the right man who knew the right man . . . and so on. In this case, the right man was "Deshbandu" Chitta Ranjan Das, an ardent nationalist and leader of the Bengal Swaraj party. (It was Das's admirers who had conferred the honorific name on him—Deshbandu, the country's friend.) Das alternated between a hard and soft line toward the British. Now he was in his soft-line period. He thought Nehru could be of most use working inside the British establishment—the ruling circles. Das talked to Sir Grimwood Mears, chief justice of the Allahabad high court and a frequent guest in the Abode of Bliss. The justice, in turn, appears to have talked to another influential figure, and so Nehru got the invitation to head the provincial department of education.

He turned it down. It was true that in this strategic post he may have had the ears of important Britishers and thus formed a one-man lobby to help free Gandhi. But Nehru felt that this would take too long. Gandhi's more energetic policy offered quicker results. Or did it? Nehru was not always sure. He was certain only of one thing—that the little man with the spindly legs now confined in Yeravda jail had better insight into history than anybody else.

Thus Nehru, high-spirited and strong-willed though he

was, again bowed to Gandhi. As his chela, Nehru worked tirelessly in the Allahabad Congress Committee office. He became manager of the office, but he was also secretary, telephone operator, and, occasionally, office boy. The organization was short-staffed because it lacked money and it lacked money because businessmen were stingy about donations. In theory, businessmen also wanted freedom, but they were afraid of abrupt change. Their main demand was for law and order and these were upheld by the British. Businessmen could make money under British rule.

In his limited free time, Nehru turned to his family. He had now been married for seven years, and it was with a pang that he realized his shortcomings as a family man. Consumed by the desire to help the country, he had little time to help his family. Was it his duty to spend so much time on public business at the expense of his kin? He decided to slow down his office work and take a good look at his private life. In doing so, he found that his wife ardently desired to become his partner in freedom's cause. He discovered that she not only had definite ideas about public affairs but also profound ideals. "She wanted," he noted, "to play her own part in the national struggle and not be merely a hanger-on and a shadow of her husband. She wanted to justify herself to her own self as well as to the world."

Then there was Indira, a beautiful child, with her large and clever eyes reflecting sadness. After returning from town, the father could barely take his eyes off the child. "Sad eyes," he would whisper. "Sad eyes," he would repeat. Then his eyes fell on the mirror he was facing. "Mine are sad eyes, too," he would say. It was evidently in the family. Yet, had they the justification to feel sad? They had no financial worries, and the home atmosphere was serene. "Sad eyes, hers and mine," Jawaharlal would meditate. "Why?" He knew the answer. For years he had been an only child in an environment where usually families were large. "Indira is the only child in this house and that is why her eyes are sad." It was hard to find playmates for the girl in a setting where the rich were few and the poor many. The chasm between the two was extremely great, and they lived—as it were—on different planets. Because of the vast difference in backgrounds, neither side felt at ease in the other's company. But basically, Indira's eyes were sad because of India's plight.

Sadness also shrouded the Nehru household for other reasons. Jawaharlal's mother was ill, and the ailment left its trace on her formerly attractive features. Sickness was, of course, the permanent partner of the elderly but, strangely, it seemed to affect the wealthy more than the poor. The latter had to keep on working, and sometimes they could forget about their poor health. But the household of a rich man was swarming with servants. There was nothing for the lady of the house to do, and she must have felt very useless. Since politics was the very air the Nehrus inhaled, the old lady's thoughts turned in that direction, too. Possessing the family's indomitable will, she also wanted to contribute to the success of their common cause.

There had been occasions when the Abode of Bliss lived up to its name. On May 10, 1921, joyous wedding music had enlivened the house when Jawaharlal's sister Swarup was married to a promising Allahabad attorney, Ranjit Pandit. Swarup, eleven years younger than Jawaharlal, had always been a stunning beauty, but, at twenty-one she was more attractive than ever. She had been educated by private tutors, and had the keen mind as well as the strong will of the Nehrus. Her

will and political articulateness made her a candidate for the
occupancy of prison cells. In due time she would be sentenced
to three jail terms, and be proud of them. Such prison sentences were to become prerequisites in later years for rising
high in the affairs of a new India.

Her husband was an attractive man. Politics was in his
blood, too, and jail terms were in his future. His mind had
a sharpness that qualified him for a place of honor in the
Allahabad Abode of Bliss, and in the political prisoners'
cells. There was no shortage of politically educated people in
the Nehru household. Pandit was an outstanding attorney. He
had a strongly developed taste for art and a love of music,
and was an accomplished linguist.

Tradition still played a role in the wedding, even though
both bride and groom had a modern outlook on life. The
relatives and kinsfolk had to be humored. The day selected
for the ceremony was the anniversary of the great Indian
Mutiny in 1857, the uprising against the British rule. Friends
predicted that India would rise against the alien regime during
the wedded life of the Nehru girl and young Pandit. They
did not predict, however, that some of the participants in this
family ceremony would play historic roles in the world.

After his rejection of a post in the provincial administration, Jawaharlal decided to strike out on a new path. In jail
he had read books about the *narodniks,* educated Russians
who, in the days of czarist rule, went among the *muzhiks,*
the peasants, to become acquainted with their ways. The
narodniks wished to see what the real Russia looked like.
Occasionally they would teach the illiterate muzhiks how to
read and write. Jawaharlal decided to become a narodnik,
an itinerant in search of the wisdom of the common folk.
If need be, he would also become a teacher.

Since the Main Street of India was the mighty Ganges, the sacred river, Nehru started his pilgrimage along its banks. He paid countless visits to the *bustees* of the plains, the poorest sections, and avoided the dwellings of the well-to-do. Then he veered southward, striking out along the Godavari, the sacred stream in central India. In his wanderings he came across the Pushkaram, the great bathing festival held at Rajahmundry every twelve years. There again he saw the heavy hand of tradition in the crowds that swarmed toward the stream in search of moral purification and a privileged position in a life after death. Hundreds of pilgrims were trampled to death on the riverbanks. Nehru was revolted by these "religious ceremonies," in which people gave evidence of their utter selfishness.

Moving south, he reached Indian states where people no longer spoke the languages based on Sanskrit, the mother tongue of Indo-European speech. There they spoke languages of the Dravidian family, such as Tamil and Telugu. As he moved from region to region, he saw for himself that India was more than a subcontinent, or a huge peninsula, that she was a world inhabited by a variety of people, following a bewildering collection of traditions and customs, believing in countless divinities, and knowing little or nothing of the world beyond their own villages.

～ FIVE ～

Chains and a New Horizon

Nehru's village explorations ended abruptly in Nabha, one of the small Indian states in the Punjab. The British had deposed its maharaja and were running the state. They were to remain in power until the maharaja's heir, Pratap Singh Malvendra Bahadur, came of age. Even though temporarily under British rule, the state was still governed under its own laws, which were extremely stringent against demonstrations. Most of the people were Sikhs, who resented the deposition of their ruler. Despite the ban, the Sikhs staged a religious demonstration. Nehru and two of his companions happened to be in Jaito, the scene of the demonstration. The authorities

Nehru in 1930. (Unless otherwise noted, all photographs courtesy United Press International.)

Above, Nehru in 1936; below, with Gandhi, 1939.

Above, Nehru in 1954; below, Nehru (extreme right) entertains visitors in New Delhi. The author is second from right. (photograph courtesy the author)

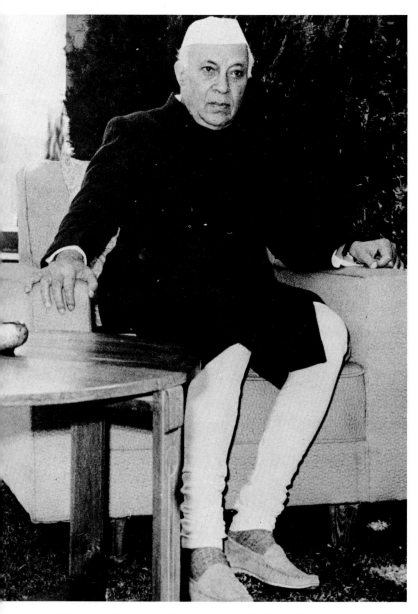

Nehru relaxes in the garden of his residence shortly before his death.

spotted them and served notice on the three to leave the place. The next train out, however, was several hours away, and no other means of transportation was available. To explain their predicament, Nehru and his companions called on the police. The official in charge could not have cared less about the fact that it was impossible to leave the state at the time ordered. He had the three men taken into custody, chained, and paraded down the streets to the railway station, there to await the train. Nehru was not sure whether he and his companions looked like monkeys, bears, or chained dogs. As prisoners, they were thrust into a crowded compartment. The train inched its way all night toward Nabha, the capital, where they were thrown into a dirty cell to spend three nights on a bare floor overrun by vermin. During those endless nights, rats swarmed over their bodies.

Then, in a filthy courtroom, the prisoners were indicted. The magistrate they faced knew no English. The official language of the court was Urdu, which the prisoners did not know very well. There were no interpreters. The trial lasted a week, during which time the judge did not write down a single line. Nehru suspected that he could not write.

During the trial another accusation was leveled against the three—conspiracy to disturb the peace of the State—even though the law said that such charges could be brought only if there were at least four participants. Soon the three defendants found themselves in the company of a fourth person, a down-at-the-heels Sikh who swore that he had been in league with them. The three had never seen him before.

During the proceedings, Nehru contracted an ailment that developed into typhus. By the time the sentences were announced—six months for the first charge, and eighteen

months for the second (two years in all)—Nehru was seriously ill. But on the same evening the sentences were
pronounced, the local British administrator suspended the
sentences, and all of them were freed.

The accused men never learned what was behind this
farce. Perhaps its object was to scare them into unquestion-
ing obedience. Or perhaps the British magistrate had discovered that Nehru was the son of one of the most illustrious
trial lawyers in the land. Still another possibility was that the
illiterate local magistrate may have overstepped the boundaries set by the British.

It tok Nehru a month to recover from his sickness. He
had learned from his experience that there was no protection
for the common man in the backward native states, which
were no better—and perhaps worse—than the regions under
direct British control.

At this time, Nehru's wife had entered a hospital. Her
case was diagnosed by the family physician, Dr. M. A. Ansari,
as advanced tuberculosis. In 1926, before the age of miracle
drugs, TB was a highly dangerous disease. It was decided to
send Kamala to Switzerland, where important pioneering
work was being done in treating the illness. The whole
family, with the exception of Nehru's parents, accompanied
her.

They embarked on a P. & O. liner at Bombay early in
March, a time when the heat of India begins to sear the
skin. On the ship, Indira, now eight, became the passengers'
darling, always the first to spot the flying fish and the last to
go to bed. With her keen mind, she startled dignified I.C.S.
officials returning to England. She was precocious and politi-
cal-minded.

"Why did you put my father in jail?" she asked, insisting on an answer. Embarrassed silence greeted her question.

"He is a good man," she continued, "a very good father, and he likes other children, too."

Gradually, her questions pierced even the most impenetrable bureaucratic armor.

When told that the official had not sent her father to jail, she insisted to him, "You did, and don't do it again." Officials, who now entered into the spirit of the game, promised that it was not going to be done again.

The family disembarked at Venice and took a train to the Swiss mountain village of Montana, which is surrounded by Alpine peaks with picturesque names—Wild Horn, Golden Horn, Broad Horn, and Balm Horn. Indira was taken to a boarding school while Nehru took Kamala to a sanatorium for TB patients, and for a time stayed with her. After a while he left, as she needed the most complete rest and special treatment. By now it was spring, the glorious awakening of nature in the Alps. Kamala watched it from the slope of a peak surrounded by the Horns. Down in the Rhone valley, she saw a land of luscious green. As the days grew warmer, the green began to climb the mountain slopes. As it climbed higher, it spread the scent of early spring. Headily scented flowers burst out of their winter abodes. Under the thawed crust of the earth, the blooms turned their radiant faces toward the sun. Daily Kamala noticed the advance of spring toward the peak. After a while, the sanatorium was surrounded by ecstatic plant life. These were good weeks for Kamala, happy and optimistic. Although there could be no doubt about the nature of her ailment, she shared the optimism of TB patients, stimulated by the fever in her body.

The Nehrus hoped that hers would not be a really serious case or that the Montana sanatorium experts might find a cure. Comforting letters from the family kept her in good spirits.

Meanwhile, Nehru was off on a business tour of Europe— a continent in which new hope was stirring. The hatreds generated by World War I were yielding to a spirit of understanding among peoples who were once foes. A Congress of Oppressed Nationalities met in Brussels; Nehru represented India, the largest of these national groups. What could they do to acquire independence? Perhaps they could unite in fighting their imperialist masters. Nehru had his doubts as he listened to speaker after speaker. Each of them thought that he had the magic power to translate bondage into independence, and to do it by words. They seemed incapable of united action.

From Brussels, Nehru went on a more extended tour of Europe, consulting the sages of the West. One of these was the famous French writer, Romain Rolland, whose home in the Swiss town of Villeneuve was a place of pilgrimage for people from India. It was Rolland who had "discovered" Gandhi for the Western world, and now Nehru wanted Rolland's ideas about the course that India should take to free itself. While in Brussels, Nehru had called upon the German playwright Ernst Toller, who had tried his hand at social reconstruction in his native Bavaria, and who was full of hope for the day when man everywhere would be his own master. Toller made a lasting impression on the visiting Indian. Nehru also called upon political leaders on the continent and in Britain to sound out their ideas on the problems of India.

In those days there was hope in Europe that the world would at long last learn to live in peace and freedom. Nehru was impressed by what he saw and heard; but he was dismayed by the chasm between the lot of his people and of those of the Western world. He saw no starvation in the West, where the people knew how to smile and laugh. In contrast, he recalled his countrymen's sad faces. In Europe, he also learned about the increasing importance of the New World across the ocean. The United States was in the midst of an unprecedented wave of prosperity. Because of that, Nehru did not think that the world's poorest citizens, the people of India, could learn much from the world's richest people, and so he had no thought of visiting America.

On the other hand, he was greatly interested in Soviet Russia. "I am very far from being a Communist," he observed later. "My roots are still perhaps partly in the nineteenth century, and I have been too much influenced by the humanist liberal tradition to get out of it completely. . . . I dislike also much that has happened in Russia, and especially the excessive use of violence in normal times." Still, he considered communism a notable experiment.

The Soviet Union appeared to him in a different light than to most people in the West. He liked to hear the Soviets call upon the oppressed people to strike off their fetters; Indians thought of themselves as the most abused victims of imperialism. Nehru was impressed by the drive of the Soviets to scrap the past (which turned out later to be a failure)—and to build a more promising future. There was much crudity and cruelty in the Soviets, but basic changes required drastic means. The present was dark, but the future was lighted with hope. "Soviet Russia," he commented, "despite certain unpleasant aspects, attracted me greatly and seemed to hold forth a message of hope to the world."

Would Nehru visit the Soviets? He hesitated for a time. Meanwhile, his father had joined the family in Europe. In the midst of his hesitations, he and his father received an invitation from the Russian government to pay a visit to Moscow. The Soviet Society for Cultural Relations with Foreign Countries was to be their host. The Nehrus accepted the invitation.

They took a train in Berlin and soon were on their way to the Soviet Union. It was a slow ride across the monotonous plains of eastern Germany, the entire width of Poland, and Russia's western marshes. Large streamers of red cloth welcomed them at the frontier: THE SOVIET PEOPLE GREET THEIR GUESTS. Their hosts wished to convey the impression that the guests had entered a new civilization in which the lowly were to be the lordly and the lordly were to become the lowly; a civilization in which there was opportunity for all, and privilege for none. The Nehrus were treated as Very Important Persons, taken on a grand conducted tour, during which they were shown aspirations ready to become realities. Although Jawaharlal Nehru was particularly sympathetic to the idea of the underdog becoming the top dog, his keen eyes detected many flaws in Russia. The tinsel flaunted before his eyes did not cover the shabbiness of life. But the Nehrus conceded that the Russian achievements could not be measured by the standards of the past. Never in history had such a gigantic experiment been undertaken in so vast a country. Just then the Soviets had passed through a period of transition when they had been afflicted by all the plagues of the world—wars, revolutions, counterrevolutions, foreign invasions, and the most awful drought in memory, which devastated their most productive fields.

The Russian rulers sympathized with India's plight. They claimed that they represented the advance guard, fighting colonial powers in the interest of the poor and hungry. They were set to start a momentous experiment—the Five-Year-Plans—under which the country was to rid itself of disease, ignorance, and poverty. The aim of the Soviet leaders was to "overtake and surpass" the United States in the production of material goods. Much of this appealed to the Nehrus, who by then were inclined to overlook the seamy side of Russian life.

From Russia, Jawaharlal Nehru returned to the Swiss sanatorium and found his wife's health much improved. As a consequence, he felt more relaxed, ready to have a fling. He went on a skiing expedition with friends in the Alps. The weather was radiant, the freshly fallen snow enticing. One of his companions was too playful, and Nehru, coming from a warm country, had no skiing experience. The careless companion gave him a shove, not realizing that Nehru was teetering on the edge of a precipice of several hundred feet of craggy rocks. At the last minute he grabbed the trunk of a tree, and was hauled back to safety. That was his last attempt at skiing.

Nehru spent the next months traveling, relaxing, discussing politics. Then, one day, the Nehrus saw an inconspicuous press dispatch that meant a great deal to them. It said that the prime minister of Britain, Stanley Baldwin, had appointed Sir John Simon, a prominent member of Parliament, to head an Indian Statutory Commission to look into the condition of India and make recommendations for change. This told the

Nehrus that the British had taken notice of India's plight, and that their work may not have been in vain. They thought it was essential for them to be at home when the Simon commission showed up on its fact-finding mission.

Indira had been placed in a girls' school in the Rhone valley town of Bex, where she was studying French. She did not particularly care for the school and wanted to return to the Abode of Bliss. Kamala's health appeared to be improving. The Nehrus had contemplated a European stay of six months, and had been abroad for nearly two years. They decided to return home, except for Motilal, who wanted to stay a while longer.

On an early morning in December, 1927, the Nehru clan moved up the gangplank of another P. & O. liner, at the French Mediterranean port of Marseilles. The Nehrus were among the last to reach the ship, the railing of which was festooned by first-class passengers; some were returning Indian Civil Service officials, others affluent Indians. These passengers could not have foreseen what roles the members of the family hurrying up the gangplank were to play in history. They could not have foreseen that the handsome young man with the doleful air was to become, one day, the first prime minister of an independent India; that the attractive child skipping up the bridge was also to become the prime minister of her country; and that the beautiful young woman, the young man's sister, was also to play a featured part on the international stage.

After their long voyage across the torrid seas, the Nehrus did not disembark, as customary, at Bombay, but proceeded instead to Colombo, the capital of the island of Ceylon. From there they continued to the mainland, and took the overnight express to Madras, where the Congress party was holding its annual session. Nehru was back in the midst of his political work.

At the Congress session, the words "Simon commission" were on everybody's lips. Nehru was full of ideas and eager to act boldly. He surprised the Congress by presenting a resolution at the meeting in which he demanded complete independence for the Indian people. That was more than any other leader had asked. To many, complete independence seemed a utopian idea. It appeared to everyone then that the subcontinent was the pivot of British might, and that if the English lost it, they would cease to be a world power. And what would happen to the hundreds of native princes with their special rights? They would fight the very thought of an independent India in which they would have to relinquish their privileges. They were princes first and Indians afterward.

Gandhi was the leader of the Congress party and the "conscience of India," known now to all as the Mahatma, the designation given to him by Rabindranath Tagore, India's Nobel Prize poet. Gandhi now more than ever considered the younger Nehru his disciple, the closest to him of all the party members. This time, however, he chided the younger man for his haste in presenting the independence resolution.

"You are going too fast," he said. "The differences between you and me appear to be so vast and so radical that there seems to be no meeting ground between us. I cannot conceal from you my grief that I should lose a comrade so valiant, so faithful, so able and so honest, as you have always been . . ."

Gandhi thought that Nehru had been too rash in defining

independence as the aim of the Congress party at a time
when the people were not yet ready for it. Such actions, he
said, put the foe on the alert and thus jeopardized the people's
cause. Nehru's greatness was manifested in his reactions to
these strong words. He took no offense, and Gandhi held no
grudge against him.

Nehru's trip to Europe taught him the lesson that a
political movement must have an organized base. In Britain,
he saw that the organized base of the Labour party was the
Trade Union Congress, the organization of industrial workers.
India's industries were not large in comparison with Britain's
but they, too, had a Trade Union Congress, T.U.C., which
Jawaharlal now began to cultivate. Quickly he rose to the top
and was elected its president. Now he had his own base from
which to operate.

Sir John Simon arrived in India with his commission to
inquire into the country's troubles. The group landed at
Bombay on February 8, 1928. They were to gather material
by traveling all over the land. Their arrival came during a
singularly hectic period in Nehru's life.

The people of India did not think much of the Simon
commission, which did not even have an Indian member.
The "reception committee" at the Gateway of India was
noisy. Demonstrators waved the black flag of sorrow and
warned Sir John to go home. When the reception became
noisy, the police stepped in wielding their heavy lathis. The
demonstration was exceptionally shrill in Madras and Lahore.
A tragic event in the latter city had a profound effect on
Nehru's life. A leader of the demonstration in that Punjabi
city was Lala Lajpat Rai (Lalaji), an elderly man and one
of the Congress stalwarts, known also as the Lion of the
Punjab. In spite of his nickname, Lalaji was a man of peace.

He wanted to protest against the composition of the commission, but he exhorted his followers to do it with dignity. However, the sight of the hated lathis enraged the demonstrators, and a wild melee ensued, with Lalaji in the middle. Precisely because he was well known in town, the police concentrated their attacks on him in the lathi charge. He was badly mauled, and died a few days later as a result of his wounds. Now the cause of India freedom had a prominent martyr, one who was close to Nehru, too. Jawaharlal fell into a dark mood in the wake of this tragic event, which was to haunt him for years to come.

"To think," he wrote, "that even the greatest of our leaders, the foremost and most popular man in the Punjab, could be so treated, seemed little short of monstrous and a dull anger spread all over the country, especially in North India. How helpless we were, how despicable, when we could not even protect the honor of our chosen leader."

Subsequently, police brutality hit Nehru directly. The episode took place in Lahore at another demonstration directed against the Simon commission. Since demonstrations had been prohibited by the police, Nehru and his friends hit upon a new idea. They could not call a mass meeting, so they organized small batches of people to move toward the center of town in a leisurely and apparently peaceful way. They converged in the main public square, where the real demonstration was to take place. Nehru was the leader of one such group, but the police were prepared for him. Mounted constables rushed out of a side street, and began flailing away at the demonstrators with lathis. The impact was so unexpected that the protesters scattered and fled. At first Nehru thought of leaving, too, but he changed his mind. As the leader, he decided to face the consequences. He stood his ground before the enraged police and took many vicious blows. Yet, he remained uncrushed psychologically as well as physically.

"The bodily pain I felt," he commented later, "was quite forgotten in a feeling of exhilaration that I was physically strong enough to face the lathi blows. And a thing that surprised me was that right through the incident, even when I was being beaten, my mind was quite clear and I was consciously analyzing my feelings."

The following day, Nehru was in another section of north India, in Lucknow, closer to home. Again he participated in a demonstration against the Simon commission, and again he was the victim of a lathi attack. This time he noticed the distorted features of the police, and for a moment he had an impulse to hit back with his fist. Then he recalled the teachings of Gandhi, and repressed his impulse.

Other forces of protest, too, were released by the general unrest. Industrial workers streamed into the streets to demand a living wage. Strikes erupted all over the country, especially around the large industries in the cities of the Ganges plains. India's largest industries, among them the Tata Iron and Steel Works at Jamshedpur, the East Indian Railways, and the Bengal Jute Works, were shut down. Even the untouchables of Calcutta entered the strike.

As president of the trade unions, Nehru was swept into the whirlpool of industrial strife. Investigating the causes of the unrest, he found his own countrymen, rich industrialists and family friends, paying their workers miserably low wages.

"Why do you pay your workers so poorly?" he wanted to know.

The industrialists considered him naïve. They did not pay their workers poorly; they paid the going rates.

"Both for patriotic and humanitarian reasons," Nehru pleaded, "you should pay them better. We cannot have a successful country if it is inhabited by people with not enough to eat."

Noticing that patriotism and humanitarianism made no impression on the industrialists, Nehru shifted his stand.

"You want to sell your products, of course. Who is going to buy them? The people. How can they buy them if they have no purchasing power because of inadequate wages?"

Nehru never got an adequate answer. The more he saw of the managerial class, the more he became a socialist. The more he became a socialist, the less the managers believed that he was one.

"He is young," they said, "and his family is rich."

He was no longer that young, and he meant what he said.

At the Lahore Congress, the greatest honor was bestowed upon Nehru, now forty years old. He was elected president of the Indian National Congress in December, 1929. The Congress represented India in its struggle for freedom. As the president-elect he mounted a white charger, riding at the head of the presidential procession, while tens of thousands cheered wildly and his mother showered flowers on her son. He was not hesitant in expressing his beliefs in his presidential address:

"I must frankly confess that I am a socialist and a republican, and am no believer in kings and princes, or in the order which produces the modern kings of industry who have greater power over the lives and fortunes of men than even the kings of old, and whose methods are as predatory as those of the feudal aristocracy. . . ."

As president of the party expressing the aspirations of the people of India, Nehru became even more of an international figure than he had been before. Now he became an Indian sage, affectionately called *Panditji,* an oracle whose words were carefully weighed. That he was a Brahman, and a Kashmiri one as well, seemed also to have counted in his favor. Nehru disliked that aspect of his popularity among the Hindus of India. What difference did his caste make? Yet, it did make a difference, even to Gandhi. It was a tradition, part of the Indian way of life. And it made a lot of difference to the country people that a Brahman was joining in common cause with them, the lower castes and outcastes. This enhanced their confidence in their future.

When a person becomes popular in India his name is enshrined in verse and song. Songs were written about Jawaharlal Nehru, the new Krishna, the godlike creature leading the charge against the evil forces of oppression and greed. A Nehru legend was in the making. He was called *Bharat Bhushan*—the Jewel of India—and hailed as *Tyagamurti*— Embodied Sacrifice, a reference to his days in jail. The younger people in the Nehru household took this in their stride. Instead of calling him by name, they would ask teasingly: "What time is it, O Indian Jewel?" or "Please pass the salt, O Embodied Sacrifice!"

Motilal, too, played an important role in the Indian freedom movement. He had been president of the Indian National Congress. For years, however, he had made no attempt to keep in step with his son who, he thought, was moving too fast. Motilal had been more of a gradualist. But now he too was gripped by the spirit of the younger generation, and soon father and son were moving together. In recognition of this fact, Motilal deeded his house to the national cause. The Abode of Bliss was renamed Abode of Independence—*Swaraj Bhawan.* It remained the office of the Congress party for years, housing its permanent body—the

All-India Congress Committee—which carried on the administrative functions between the annual sessions. The Nehrus moved into another, even larger, house, next to the old one, and called that estate the Abode of Bliss. Anand Bhawan and Swaraj Bhawan were now next-door neighbors. This proximity stimulated even more political activity in the Nehru household. What was more natural than that callers at the Abode of Independence should also pay their respects at the Abode of Bliss? And what was more natural than that the dwellers in the Abode of Bliss should maintain close contact with their former home?

Because the work of the National Congress was so closely integrated with the life of the Nehrus, it was also natural that the political work of the family should now spread to the women, even to Kamala, in spite of her illness. Because of her resilience and willpower, she felt neither pain nor fatigue for long periods of time. The slight fever of the TB patient became a stimulant in bursts of activity that surprised even the Nehru household. Carried away by the feverish activity of the older ones, little Indira, too, threw herself into the political movement. She recruited children of the neighborhood into a "Monkey Brigade," whose members performed useful work for the common cause. They picketed stores selling foreign goods; freed adults from routine jobs; and sneaked messages past British guards. During one of the mass demonstrations in Allahabad, when the police were clubbing the protesters, Indira rushed up to a police stalwart wielding his lathi. "Beat me," she cried, "take me to jail."

The independence movement was reaching its climax. It did so at the annual meeting of the Congress party in December, 1929, held in Lahore. The party declared the independence of India, and designated January 26, as National

Independence Day. This was, of course, a one-sided declaration which the British authorities ignored. But, while they could ignore the declaration of independence, they could not ignore subsequent events, culminating in the Great Salt March, which projected India into the forefront of world attention.

SIX

More Jails and Nationalist Fervor

Gandhiji, as many people called the Great Soul with profound respect, hit upon an idea to dramatize India's plight and give substance to the declaration of independence. The British had placed a tax on salt, which even the poorest had to pay. This aroused Gandhi, who now called upon his countrymen to refuse to pay the salt tax as a first step in implementing the declaration. He announced that he would lead a group of protesters to the sea, as a symbolic gesture. The march attracted chroniclers of contemporary history from all parts of the world. On March 12, 1930, Gandhi, sixty-one years old, set out, staff in hand, on the historic pilgrimage from his *ashram,* his place of meditation, a shrine near the town of Sabarmati. At first, he was accompanied by seventy-nine volunteers. They headed westward to the sea, two hundred miles away. Hundreds and then thousands joined him on this journey to the sea, which lasted twenty-five days. He had the attention of the world when he picked up a handful of brine on the seashore at the town of Dandi. At the same time, he called on his countrymen to pay no tax on salt. Thus, he flouted what he considered an unjust law. He was subsequently arrested, and placed in jail. There was no trial.

At first, Jawaharlal Nehru thought little of the Great Salt March, which he considered melodramatic and a publicity stunt. But he changed his mind when he observed the world's reaction. Melodramatic the salt march was, but—Nehru had to concede—it was most effective, and an eye-opener to millions. The Indian National Congress had worked ceaselessly to call attention to the Indian freedom movement. Yet, tens of millions of people in India had never heard of its work. The salt march publicized its aims. "What a wizard the little man is," Nehru had to admit, "the conscience of India. More than anybody else he knows how to arouse the conscience of the world."

Gandhi also aroused the British, since all over India the salt-tax law was violated. The authorities then undertook one of the greatest manhunts in the history of the country. The British decided to paralyze the freedom movement, and the great roundup began.

Nehru was one of the Congress leaders to be apprehended. He was on his way to the train for a trip to Raipur in the Central Provinces, on April 14, 1930, when he felt the familiar police "greeting," a hand on his right shoulder.

"You are under arrest," the constable said in his routine

voice. He must have uttered the same phrase thousands of times in the last few days. All the higher echelon of the Congress party was arrested for violation of the tax law, and many members of the lower echelons, too—thousands, at first, then tens of thousands. It is estimated that about one hundred thousand were detained. The problem which the British now faced was—how were they to jail the countless thousands of people? Was India to be turned into a huge detention pen?

Charged with the violation of the salt-tax law, Nehru was sentenced to six months in jail, his fourth prison term. He was taken to the Naini Central Prison in the Himalaya foothills in the United Provinces. In years to come he was to be intimately acquainted with the place. Nehru was placed at first in that part of the jail reserved for dangerous criminals, called *kuttaghar* (doghouse), the maximum security section of the jail. The doghouse was a prison within a prison, a drab structure with four cells within a circular space, surrounded by a wall fifteen feet high, which was surrounded by still another wall. Although Naini is situated at an elevation of some six thousand feet, the summer days in the cell were stiflingly hot. Eventually, Nehru was granted the privilege to sleep outside the cell, but within the enclosure, surrounded by the wall. Throughout his term, he was to receive privileges he did not seek. He got them, probably, because his jailers could not help seeing in him the Cambridge graduate, the cultured Englishman. His first language was English, the jailers' native tongue, and his education was, no doubt, superior to theirs.

In prison, Nehru again came into contact with common criminals. Prisoners were identified by wooden boards attached to their right shoulders, which provided informa-

tion about their sentences. The anticipated date of release for
one of them was 1996—almost seventy years later. The face
of this elderly man was a tale of tragedy. Tragedy was also
written on many other faces. Life in the jail meant an endless procession of nightmares, and Nehru felt that death
would have spelled salvation for many. Although he was
against capital punishment, he felt that for some of the
prisoners, a quick death on the gallows would have been a
blessing.

What were the crimes of the convicts? A large number
of them, young boys in their teens, may have been caught
stealing food for starving relatives. Others were *dacoits,*
or gangsters; they were feared and detested. They gave the
impression of being strong-willed, pugnacious people who
had become dacoits because they had been entrapped by life,
on the point of starvation. They had smashed their way out of
this entrapment. There was no excuse for their actions, Nehru
admitted, but under different circumstances, and in a different
environment, these people might have become successful
members of society. Hunger-ridden India was a breeding
ground of crime.

Each prisoner had permission to write a letter every three
months. Since most prisoners did not know how to write, the
politicals helped them. Often the illiterate prisoners did not
know the addresses of their kin. Were they merely stupid
people? Not at all. They lived in a society in which their
addresses were the gutters. They could not engage in conversation about anything. They could talk only about the
"injustice" that landed them in their hopeless plight. Education might have given them subjects fit for conversation, but
education had not been theirs.

One day, the prison grapevine transmitted the news to the

Naini doghouse that new prisoners were to arrive. Some of them were said to be of great prominence. On a heavy monsoon day a large group arrived, including his own father. Motilal had not been warned about the surprise in store for him, and his momentary happiness tied his tongue. The father, too, had been sentenced to six months in jail.

"We two jailbirds," he told his son, "will make a happy team. What a family! Both father and son fit for prison. We shall turn this cell-block of Naini Tal prison into the Anand Bhawan of the Himalayas—the Abode of Bliss."

"I don't know what to say," his son countered. "Shall I say that I am happy to see you? That is not the way for the son to welcome his father within the prison walls."

Motilal roared with laughter. For a moment he was the old Motilal, master of the situation.

"I'll join you," he answered, "in your activities. What do you do here all day long, these weeks and months?"

"I am taking a post-graduate course in politics. I am also planning how to become a more effective member of the Congress party."

"I am your fellow student," Motilal answered, with a grin.

Taking a better look at his father after the first flush of pleasure, Nehru was less delighted. Motilal, now approaching seventy, looked very old. He tired quickly, and he was a sick man. To make things worse, the heavy monsoon rains damaged the cell-block ceiling, and the two men had to be assigned to separate cells. The authorities, too, grew concerned about Motilal's health, realizing that his life was ebbing away. His temperature went up rapidly; his weight down.

Meanwhile, the British government in London began to

have second thoughts. Business in Britain was poor and unemployment chronic. India was boycotting British goods, and other countries, especially Japan, were making inroads into the peninsular trade.

Lord Irwin was the viceroy in India and he received word from London to try to reach an agreement with the Congress leaders. The viceroy's offer was vague—a "freer India in due time" with dominion status. Canada was a dominion and its status was desirable from the Indian point of view, but when could such status be reached?

Irwin's offer was presented to Gandhi, the Nehrus, and other leaders. A conference was to be called to discuss the question. Before that, the British insisted, the civil-disobedience campaign must be stopped. Should the leaders of India call off the campaign? That was the question they had to answer.

Their discussion took place in jails. Gandhi and some other leaders were in Yeravda; the Nehrus in Naini Tal. A "little round table conference" was called to help Gandhi give his answer.

The hosts were the prison authorities. Considerately, they inquired about the kind of drinks that the Nehrus liked. They liked tea, a national drink. What type of tea? Motilal liked the Darjeeling kind, and that was served. The round table was placed in the prison yard, and the conferences were convened after the twilight hours had started to waft the spice-scented mountain breezes from the peaks. The jail was situated on a spur of the range, and the air was so crystalline that Nehru thought he could touch the snow-covered flanks of the mountain giants. There were pleasant talks in the cool evening, and the Nehrus forgot temporarily that they were surrounded by prison walls. Motilal favored the talks with the British, but his son was hesitant. It was suggested that they meet with Gandhi at Yeravda, near Poona and south of Bombay.

The British ordered a special train to take their Naini prisoners to Yeravda, but to avoid a public demonstration they made no announcement of the trip. The prisoners were accompanied by the highest Naini prison official, Lieutenant Colonel Martin. In order to escape attention, the train was to bypass scheduled stops at Delhi, Ahmedabad, Baroda, and Bombay, and was to halt only at wayside stations for refueling.

But the wayside stations were jammed with crowds. Martin was mystified. Had the news leaked out, alerting the people? The prisoners themselves were at a loss to understand the mystery, and they suspected the grapevine. Curious officials inquired of Indians, who responded with a mysterious grin. "One feels such things," some of them said. Some of the more mystical-minded had a ready answer. "We followed the 'radiance.' It showed the way to us." More sophisticated people smiled quizzically. "This is the inscrutable Orient, you know."

The train did not even stop at Poona, a large city, but it did stop at the small town of Kirkee. And again there was the vast crowd, not only men but also women, some of them holding infants aloft to expose them to the darshana. In the action of the mothers there was the ardent hope that their infants might grow to manhood in an India in which people had enough to eat.

The gate of Yevrada Prison was thown open and the Naini prisoners were ushered into the cell of the Great Soul. Gandhi, happy to see his friends, appeared to be in top form. Four other Indian leaders played leading roles at this conference. Vallabhbhai Patel, who was to become a political leader of independent India in years to come; Madame Sarojini Naidu, a prominent leader of Indian women; Dr. Syed Mahmud, a leader in the province of Bihar; and Jairamdas Doulatram, a party strategist.

The uniqueness of the occasion amused Gandhi; and his mischievous eyes lit up with pleasure as he greeted his guests in this "office" cell. There he had a full-time secretary —a Congress official and fellow prisoner. Gandhi was his old self, his metal-framed eyeglasses bestriding the tip of his long nose, his puckish smile revealing the pink gums in his mouth; he did not use his dentures in the presence of friends. He had just completed the daily quota of spinning that he considered a patriotic duty, and he wore only his dhoti. There was hardly any flesh on him, but he was in good health. "Half a dozen jailbirds," he quipped, "deciding the fate of India. Let's get started."

For three days they discussed their country's plight. Civil disobedience was the strongest weapon of the movement and to reliquish it was tantamount to giving up the fight. Finally, they reached their decision.

India was to get a national government responsible to the people, and the right to secede from the empire at will. Once these terms were granted, the civil-disobedience campaign would be called off.

The British would not concede these terms. They still considered India the pivot on which the empire revolved and they were loath to relinquish their hold. While the government in London was ready to grant concessions, it was not ready to grant full independence. There was nothing to be done for the moment and the special train was ordered for the return journey. Gandhi took leave of his fellow "jailbirds," assuring them that in time they would be released if their conduct was good. Cracking jokes, with his cackling laughter, he wished them a pleasant return journey and a happy stay in jail.

Again the train schedule was kept secret and the special train stopped only at small stations for refueling. Again there were the crowds along the right of way, their presence more of a mystery than ever. And this time they were even larger.

After a lengthy journey across the plains, the special train began its puffing ascent into the Himalaya hills. Lieutenant Colonel Martin was a decent man and he was worried about Motilal's health. The long trip and the excitement of the conference had left their mark on the old man. Martin wanted to do everything in his power to make the detention more pleasant for his prisoners. Perhaps food of a different kind would be of aid to Motilal, who replied that his tastes in food were simple. But at the insistence of the prison official, he listed the dishes that he liked. As the list lengthened, the face of the colonel lengthened, too. Motilal Nehru had been too much a darling of fortune to know anything about simple foods. Only the most expensive restaurants could cater to such taste as his. The prison superintendent did what he could, but that was not too much. Unfortunately, it became clearer every day that not even the best food could have improved Motilal's declining health.

And no amount of tenderness could help. Motilal's lungs grew weaker and his fever mounted higher as he continued to lose weight. He had been in prison exactly ten weeks before the authorities became aware of the true state of his health, which he had kept from them. Now the British knew, and they did not want his death on their conscience. He was released from Naini Tal on September 8. His son, it turned out, was not to remain in jail without the companionship of a close relative. Nehru's brother-in-law, Ranjit Pandit, joined him a few days later. Not long after that, Nehru was released, having served his six-month term. However, he was not to remain free for long.

Motilal was now recuperating—or so the world thought—at Mussoorie, the family's favorite hill station in the Himalaya foothills. After his release, Nehru, with Kamala and Indira, joined him there. Indira and other Nehru children heartened their parents and grandfather by organizing patriotic meetings. They grabbed a flag of the independence movement and carried it around the house, singing *Jhanda uncha rahe hamara*—"May our flag continue to wave"—much to the chagrin of vacationing British Indian civil servants.

Nehru realized that his freedom was conditioned on his "good behavior." Yet he could not compromise his beliefs even when facing jail. So he decided to go among the peasants, who were very dissatisfied at the drop in the price of jute, which many of them produced. The authorities, aware of his plans, served notice on him under Section 144 of the Indian Criminal Procedure Code, which enjoined him from speaking in public. Promptly he proceeded from the hill station to his native Allahabad where a meeting of the kisans had been called. He spoke on the no-taxation policy. The meeting was a success, as usual. Nehru's fame by now was so great that he would have been a success even if he had recited the alphabet. From Allahabad, he and his wife were to ride to another meeting, but within sight of their house, their car was stopped. Again there was the familiar tap on the right shoulder and Nehru was a prisoner, on his way to his "home" away from home.

He left Kamala a sick woman in the advanced stages of

tuberculosis. The continuous, slow rise in her body temperature was stimulating for a time. She was now in this stimulating stage. Motilal, too, had a fever, and he, too, was optimistic, assailed only at times by doubts, especially when looking into the mirror after a sleepless night. The fever of the younger members of the household was political. Gone were the days when Indian political leaders thought that their efforts for freedom were only daydreams. Now they were certain that Britain's resistance to change was on the wane. Therefore, the political fever in the Nehru household affected everyone, even little Indira. It was a feverish household, without a doubt.

In the new Abode of Bliss, Kamala was consumed by an ambition to work for the national cause. Now that her husband spent long spells in jail she threw herself into political chores, as if propelled by the idea that she had to do his work. And so she led the women's demonstrations to boycott foreign cloth and replace it by khaddar, homespun goods. She led demonstrations for the release of Congress leaders for satyagraha.

When dealing with her, the authorities restrained themselves for a while, realizing that arresting her on political charges would give her a badge of honor. The Nehrus had already given two national heroes to the common cause, and to jail Kamala would further glorify the clan. They warned her but she ignored the warning. So on New Year's Day, 1931, they arrested her, too. Before being taken away, she was interviewed by reporters.

"I am unspeakably happy," she said, and her flushed cheeks proved it, "to follow in my husband's footsteps. I hope our people will keep the flag flying."

Nehru was proud, too, when he first heard the news,

but later he was concerned as he became fully aware of
Kamala's failing health. How would the rigors of jail affect
her? Later he learned that the prison authorities were making
Kamala's stay in jail tolerable.

What about little Indira? A visitor to the Nehru home in
those days recalls being confronted by the grave-faced child.
"I am sorry, papa and mama are not home," she said. "Both
of them are in jail."

Again, the child tried to get jailed by taking her mother's
admonition literally, waving the Indian national flag and
carrying it into the crowded Allahabad bazaar at the head of
a children's parade. But Indira had not yet reached the age
to be taken to jail.

Meanwhile, the authorities adopted a new policy toward
some political prisoners—young men of lower social status.
They found that the Congress party glorified prison cells and
that many young people who wanted to gain status were
determined to go to jail. The British, wishing to discourage
them, determined to turn the detention pens into places of
shame. With that in mind, they introduced the disciplinary
punishment of flogging, which they carried out in a particularly degrading way. People of Nehru's stature were
immune, however, to such humiliations. In protest against the
floggings, Nehru and the older prisoners went on a hunger
strike. Jawaharlal was not an ascetic, and going without food
was a real hardship for him, but he managed not to eat for
seventy-two hours. As a result of the hunger strike, flogging
in Naini jail was discontinued.

Motilal remained at home, no longer able to engage in
work because of his health. He did visit his son in jail and
now Jawaharlal was truly shocked. What had happened to the
vigorous man with the roaring voice, his earthshaking

laughter and Olympian explosions of wrath? Now he was subdued, all skin and bones; his face ashen; his hair completely gray. No physician was needed to tell the son that Motilal would not live for long, even though he was trying to play the healthy man.

Meanwhile, the British had gone ahead with their plan for a Round Table Conference in London to prepare the way for a freer India—a federation with a measure of self-government. It took some time for them to persuade Gandhi and the Nehrus to consider their plan, for the Indian leaders wanted full independence. But, eventually, an agreement was reached.

"His Majesty," said the official notices, "graciously consented" to the release of Gandhi and Nehru. Kamala was released, as well as thirty high-ranking political prisoners. In turn, the party leaders called off the civil-disobedience campaign. This was preliminary to the second round table conference in which Gandhi was to speak for the Congress party. The prisoners were released on January 26, 1931. The words "round table" indicated that all the participants were to be considered equal. The table, which must have been huge indeed to accommodate more than a hundred participants, had neither head nor foot. The government representatives were considered equal to the delegates of India—Hindus, Muslims, untouchables, and native princes. Some of the latter were probably the richest people of the country; many of the former were the poorest of the world.

After Nehru's release and the convening of the second round table conference, a great sorrow overwhelmed the family and India. Motilal reached the last stage of a historic journey that had elevated him to one of the greatest men of India. And to the end, he did not know how sick he was. Shortly before his son's release, he wrote, "I was getting on more or less satisfactorily until yesterday when there was a relapse and I spent the whole night without a wink. . . . But I hope I shall have a better night. It is a satisfactory feature that my weight is steadily maintained and stands at one hundred and nineteen pounds today."

To his son in jail, that was not a satisfactory feature. He recalled his father in his prime, the picture of health and vigor, now satisfied with the weight of a youngster. Motilal was in Lucknow in the house of the Raja of Kalakandar, under the care of specialists. He was still optimistic when his physicians had abandoned hope. On the morning of February 6, 1931, his condition took a turn for the worse; and in the afternoon it became alarming. At 6:40 in the evening, he died.

The scene at the bedside was moving. The former beauty queen, Swaruprani, was a pathetic figure. Wearing her round, black-rimmed eyeglasses to conceal her tears, her looks reflected inexpressible grief. Nehru himself looked haggard and thin, while Indira was dissolved in tears.

News of the death spread quickly, and by 7:30 in the morning of the following day, the Raja's house had become a place of pilgrimage. Draped in flowers, the body was lying in state in the central hall, and there was a continuous flow of silent mourners—prominent citizens, officials, and others. Everyone on the outside was anxious to go in, to be exposed to the departed man's blessed influence. To avoid a crush of people which may have been fatal for many, Motilal's body was taken down the Lucknow main streets so that hundreds of thousands could be blessed. The body, wrapped in the national flag, was put upon a decorated car and carried down the Rae Bareli Road on the way to Allahabad. Countless people sought to keep up with the car, to be exposed to

Motilal's aura, while other thousands looked at the cortege from windows, housetops, and every available place all along the road. Motilal's son-in-law drove the car, and behind the bier was the cortege of mourners, headed by Gandhi, who tried to comfort Swaruprani.

The body was taken to the Nehru residence in Allahabad. There, too, were countless people hoping to have the dead leader's radiance. The final trip was undertaken to the holy streams. All stores closed. "Let all of us vow," Gandhi said, "before the last remains of our great hero on the banks of the Jumna and the Ganges that we will not rest until India's freedom is achieved—freedom dear to Motilaji's heart." Annie Besant expressed the opinion of many: "He is not gone from us, though we lose sight of the body of the man we loved."

The Chief Justice of Allahabad, an Englishman, uttered this eulogy: "When I came here twelve years ago, and was beginning to learn the names and positions of the members of the Bar, I was struck by the respect and the pride with which all his colleagues spoke of Pandit Motilal Nehru. When I had the pleasure of meeting him I understood the reasons for the affection with which he was viewed. It was his goodness of heart. He had a profusion of other gifts, too: knowledge came easily to him and as an attorney he possessed the art of presenting his case in the most attractive form. Every fact fell into its proper place. He had a resonant public-speaking voice and a charm of manner that made it a pleasure to listen to him."

Now that the old lion was gone, Nehru felt a still greater obligation to work for the common cause. He felt that the fate of India was a family obligation, too. But the paths of Nehru and Gandhi still continued to diverge. Jawaharlal wanted

India's full independence immediately as a free member of the British Empire, with the right to secede. The British felt differently, they had obligations toward the native princes, the religious minorities, and the untouchables. These matters would have to be settled before independence was granted.

Gandhi turned over these things in his mind. He decided to stick to his previous line of reaching independence more gradually, giving the British time to arrange matters in accordance with their obligations.

He worked out a timetable of liberation. First, the end of oppressive measures, including general amnesty for the politicals, and the immediate end of repression. Then the return to the rightful owners of property confiscated by the government. Also, the freedom to manufacture salt and even to boycott foreign goods. Then an inquiry into police brutality.

The basic measures on Gandhi's timetable called for the granting of a constitutional government, a federation, and British safeguards in such matters as defense, foreign affairs, the status of the minorities, and credit and banking.

Several of the questions had to be answered during the negotiations, especially federation and the British safeguards. Did the British insist on retaining the right of control of India's defense and foreign affairs?

Nehru objected to some of Gandhi's ideas as being nebulous. "What frightens me," he wrote to the Mahatma, "is your way of springing surprises on us." He was even blunt with Gandhi. "Although I have known you for fourteen years," he went on, "there is something about you which I cannot understand. It fills me with apprehension."

Had they been smaller men, such words might have meant the end of their relations. But they felt free to speak so frankly because they were not small men.

Gandhi replied in his disarming way, "Yes, I admit the presence of this unknown element and confess that I myself cannot answer for it or foretell where it might lead to."

Now it was the British government's turn to come back with an answer. The answer was a measure of federation, with lots of reservations. Many things would have to be ironed out: first, the problems relating to the princely states in India; then the communities—that is, the religious question; then the problem of what the English called the scheduled classes and whom Gandhi's followers knew as the *Harijans,* children of God.

Thus, the second Round Table Conference in London was called to reach an agreement on the principal issues of the subcontinent. Before Gandhi left for London, he had to have the consent of the Congress Working Committee, many of whose members were unhappy about the "wishy-washy" compromise. Nehru was unhappiest of all, since he wanted a clearcut solution. But in the end Gandhi had his way— as he almost always did. Not that the other leaders of the movement carried no weight. Some of them were willful people, too, who fought for their views. But Gandhi had the "soul power" to make people see the light—his light. And his light illuminated the road to the Round Table Conference on India's future status in the summer of 1931.

In August, the Indian delegation, with Gandhi as the most prominent member, descended the gangplank of the Peninsular and Oriental liner *Rajputana* at a London dock. All the newspapermen, radio commentators, and cameramen seemed to have congregated at the pier to meet the frail little man with the worldwide reputation. Flashing his familiar grin, he descended the gangplank with his loping steps. With his spectacles at the very tip of his long nose, he looked more

than ever like a wise owl. He wore only his dhoti, and was
followed by some of the world's richest men, the maharajas,
nizams, and nawabs, resplendent in their silken tunics
embellished by the most expensive jewelry.

From home Nehru kept track of Gandhi's performance.
The Great Soul was surrounded by Indian princes—the Aga
Khan, the Nizam of Hyderabad, richest of the rich. Yet
Gandhi in his loincloth outshone them. The Muslim League
delegation was on hand, too, headed by Mohammed Ali
Jinnah, tall, austere, pinch-faced, and aloof, with an aristo-
cratic air. The untouchables were represented by Dr. B. R.
Ambedkar, a Harijan himself, and suspicious of the caste-
Hindus' designs. He was particularly suspicious of Gandhi
because Ambedkar was jealous of the other man's fame.
The most powerful men around the tables were not the
fabulously rich nabobs and nizams, but the British officials
with such unimpressive titles as collector and deputy collector, officials of the mighty Indian Civil Service.

Eagerly, Nehru read the reports about the London conference, and he found them disturbing. To him it seemed
that the participants followed circuitous routes leading to the
satisfaction of individual claims. One person only—Gandhi
—followed a straight line designed to lead to India's eman-
cipation.

Mohammed Ali Jinnah was concerned with the Muslims,
about one-tenth of India's total population. "What is going
to happen to them?" he asked. "Are they to be absorbed by
the Hindus?" This question disturbed Nehru. The Muslims
were Indians, just as the Hindus were. The aim was not
absorption but liberation.

The princes, too, were thinking only of themselves. They
were Indians, to be sure, and wanted to have a freer hand—

for themselves, but not for the country as a whole. "Would our domains be absorbed in an independent India?" they asked. Again Nehru replied, "Why always think of absorption? The word is liberation."

Dr. Ambedkar was concerned only with the untouchables he represented. They occupied the lowest social level; most of them had no education. They had to be given adequate representation in the projected new order. Nehru believed that this representation could be assured within the framework of a free India.

Then there were the representatives of the Sikhs. They also wanted special status for themselves. Why always "special status, special status?" Nehru kept asking himself as he followed the London news. Do not these people realize that they are playing into British hands? They provide the best illustration of the English contention that Indians are unable to find a common ground, that their interests are too diverse, their fragmentation beyond relief.

Gandhi tried to pull the threads together. First, India should be given the right to conduct its own affairs without the British overlordship. Then the special problems of the various groups could be reconciled.

Gandhi presented the issue—the gradual transfer of power to India. Nothing could be simpler than that. But simplicity yielded to complexity as each group thought and talked of itself. Gandhi seemed to dominate the scene. Whenever he spoke, a deep hush enwrapped the audience. Did he convince the participants? He did, indeed—completely, if the attention he received was the yardstick. But if one were to judge by the results, he did not. But could any earthly or even divine power convince people who did not want to be convinced? They refused to be convinced because each saw salvation only within the framework of his own group, and not within that of the entire subcontinent.

What was the end of the conference which was to write one of the most momentous chapters of history? A brief communiqué from the seat of power in London: "His Majesty's government will give serious attention to the proposals presented at the round table conference."

The camera lights were focused on Gandhi in London: all the world wanted to see and hear him. But for the people of India, the conference had failed. Yet it was not Gandhi who had failed. The vested interests of India were not ready for a solution, and the British were not willing to work against what they regarded as their own interests.

Gandhi left for the European mainland to visit people of influence who might help to facilitate the next move. Some of them were influential in launching bold, new ideas—bold and new because they were sensible and, therefore, seemingly unique and even utopian. Like Nehru, Gandhi called upon Romain Rolland, the French writer in Switzerland—a man whose pen meant much for the cause of common sense and India's new place in the world.

The "little brown man" also stopped off in Rome where he called on Benito Mussolini. Il Duce, as he was known, was not then a tyrant, and he appeared to sympathize with Gandhi's aspirations.

Nehru headed the delegation that met Gandhi at Bombay. Gandhi looked his old self, with his puckish face somewhat drawn by fatigue. Nehru looked pensive as usual.

The Congress party leaders now had to make an important decision. Before the London trip, Gandhi had called off the satyagraha—nonviolent noncooperation. Now that the Round Table Conference was over without producing results,

Nehru wanted the movement to be renewed. He won his point.

Soon afterward the authorities made large-scale arrests in Nehru's homeland, the United Provinces. He decided to return there for the intensification of satyagraha. At Bombay he took the train to Allahabad. He got off the train at the Chheoki railway station, a few miles from home, to take the shuttle to Allahabad. Suddenly a constable appeared and served a court order on Nehru, ordering him not to leave the Allahabad municipal limits for an indefinite period. It also ordered him to refrain from appearing at public functions and from contributing to printed publications. The order was signed by the British magistrate of the district. His temper afire, Nehru continued the trip to Allahabad, determined to disregard the order. Arriving at home, tired and aroused, he wrote a curt note to the magistrate, telling him that his internment order was illegal and would not be obeyed. This letter was to cost Nehru dearly.

On December 26, in complete disregard of the magistrate's order, Nehru decided to have a conference with Gandhi at Bombay and he boarded the train at Allahabad. This time he passed Chheoki station without an incident. But an incident did occur after the train had left. At the border of the Allahabad district the train stopped at the wayside station of Iradatganj. There Nehru was met by a reception committee of police constables. Unceremoniously, the policemen transferred him and his traveling companion, Tassaduk Ahmad Sherwani, president of the United Provinces Congress Committee, into the prison wagon, and took them to Naini prison.

The trials of Nehru and Sherwani took place in prison. Nehru, forty-three, was sentenced to two years' imprisonment; his companion received only six months. Their offenses were exactly the same—disobeying the district magistrate. Why then the difference in jail terms? Naturally, it was due to the curt letter to the judge.

The failure of the Round Table Conference touched off a new blaze of civil disobedience. Gandhi, too, was rearrested and lodged in Yeravda Prison. Tens of thousands of men were rounded up and imprisoned. Yet, the campaign of civil dis- obedience went on, and persons taken out of the campaign by arrests were replaced by other men and increasingly by women. In the past the authorities had been lenient with women, because for one thing, there was a shortage of jails for them. But now women were no longer spared; India began to experience a building boom in jails.

Most of the female contingent in the Nehru household now moved into the political battle: Jawaharlal's two sisters, Swarup and Krishna, together with their elderly mother. The familiar police wagon showed up again in front of the Abode of Bliss, and the Nehru women were shepherded into it. They were tried and convicted for infractions of one of the innumerable police ordinances. Each of the women re- ceived a sentence of a year in jail, but the authorities did not enforce the sentence of Nehru's mother.

Mother Nehru was affronted; she wanted to join her family in jail. A chance to win her wish came on April 6, 1932, the second anniversary of Gandhi's epic Salt March to the sea.

The anniversary was to be commemorated by a demonstra- tion in various parts of the land, including Allahabad, and Swaruprani Nehru, now a frail old woman, wanted to be part of it. Friends tried in vain to dissuade her. Since she was too weak to walk, they placed her in a wheelchair at the head of the marching. The police pounced upon the women and thrashed away with their lathis. The old woman was knocked off her chair. She lay, bruised and bleeding and unconscious on the pavement, as the police charged over her. Finally she was wheeled back to the Abode of Bliss, not seriously hurt. "A woman of iron," the neighbors marveled. But she had not managed to get into jail.

Meanwhile, after six weeks' confinement in Naini, Jawaharlal had been transferred to the jail at Bareilly in the north. There he became acquainted with another kind of jailbird. The story of these men taught Nehru a lesson about the influence of environment. The thick forest jungle, called *tarai,* in the Bareilly district was inhabited at the time by wild animals, including tigers, bears, and pigs, and by savage men descended from the warlike Rohilla Pathan clans. In the course of generations, clan members used the jungle as a sanctuary for their forays on the nearby fertile land. In this environment, they had developed criminal traits that presented grave problems to law-enforcement authorities. Several of these men were Nehru's jailmates. He tried to talk satyagraha to them, but he could not reach them; crime was their normal way of life.

In prison Nehru's thinking underwent further changes. The heat was excessive in some of his prisons, and meat spoiled quickly. Nehru contracted a stomach ailment. Brahmans are supposed to be vegetarians, but Nehru, although he was a Brahman, was not at the time a vegetarian; after this experience in prison, he became one. For reasons of health, he gave up eating meat.

In jail Nehru always followed a strict schedule of work.

While in prison, he wrote some of the books that were to enhance his fame. For relaxation, he turned to the world of nature around him. The nearby jungles were teeming with birds, and some found sanctuary in the jail. Nehru was fascinated. He found the green-feathered, red-billed parrots almost human. There was, for instance, the case of the flirtatious female parrot, courted by two aggressive males. The males fought many fights for her favors while she— thoroughly pleased with the feud—kept preening herself, and then mated with the victor.

There were also the local varieties of pigeons. Nehru liked to study their ways, too. He came to know them so well that he gave them names. He called one of them The Shy One, another The Bold One, and another The Greedy One. The one who snapped up food tendered to the others was dubbed The Gangster.

But the long spells in prison began to affect Nehru's health. The climate of Bareilly did not agree with him. The prison authorities took notice and began to treat him with some consideration. Was it because of his British education or the fame of his family? Or did his jailers treat him better because they realized that he was a unique person? His darshana may have been obvious to them, too. Whatever the reason for this differential treatment, it was decided to transfer him to a jail with better conditions.

On the morning of the day of transfer, the prison warden brought him a parcel.

"I am told that you are studying German. These are illustrated magazines in that language and I thought you might like to look at them." Nehru was touched. He had been at Bareilly for a little over four months. His transfer was effected in secrecy; the authorities were afraid that there might be a mass demonstration if the move became public knowledge. He was whisked to a small wayside station some fifty miles from town and from there the train took him to Dehra Dun, where he was to spend the longest period of his imprisonment—fourteen and a half months.

As prisons go, it was a good one. It lay close to the mountains: to the north were the Himalaya foothills, which reached an average of eight thousand feet, and to the south the Siwalik hills rose to about three thousand feet. The hills were covered by tea plantations—a prosperous district. The environment was important for Nehru, because here, too, he found more birds to marvel at. He liked to watch the ordered flight of the wild ducks, their bodies ashimmer against the sky. He became accustomed to the plaintive call of the koel, the Himalayan cousin of the European cuckoo, and to the excited trill of the brain-fever bird, a series of ascending shrill tones. The eagles and vultures interested him because of their tremendous efficiency. One of the strangest creatures he encountered at Dehra Dun was a mammal called a *bo* by the peasant who carried it past the prison gate. It was going to be turned into a tasty curry, the peasant said. To Nehru, the creature looked like a cross between a lizard and a small crocodile. Actually, it was an animal the Malayans call a pangolin, an anteating inhabitant of Asia.

Life in the Dehra Dun prison was quieter than in other jails, and Nehru had time to read. He took a deep liking to the quiet hours he spent with books. He avoided novels because, as he said, he was looking for knowledge, not for entertainment. Travel books attracted him, but mostly he was interested in politics, economics, and history.

He liked to read Marco Polo, the pioneering adventurer-traveler who remained undeterred by hardships and strange customs. Nehru was also fascinated by the narratives of the greatest of all Muslim travelers, the fourteenth-century, Tangier-born Abu Abdullah Mohammed, surnamed Ibn Batuta. This indefatigable man had traveled all over the then-known world for twenty-seven years, covering 75,000 miles, much of it on foot. He had ranged as far as India, calling on the court of Mohammed Tughlak, the sultan at Delhi. Other favorite travelers of Nehru were his own contemporaries, such as Sven Hedin, whose famous books, *Through Asia, The Silk Road, Mount Everest,* and *From Pole to Pole,* enchanted him.

Nehru's main intellectual fare was the philosophy of history. He ran into difficulties in getting a copy of Oswald Spengler's *Decline of the West,* which he was particularly anxious to read. Because of its title, the British warden thought it was a subversive book. Very much to Nehru's liking were the books of the American theologian Reinhold Niebuhr, whose *Moral Men and Immoral Society* confirmed many of Nehru's views. Nehru agreed with Niebuhr especially on the point that the modern nation demands the total devotion of its citizens—not to God what is God's and to Caesar what is Caesar's but everything to Caesar and lip service to God.

At Dehra Dun, Nehru had time, too, to delve into the ponderous *Das Kapital* of Karl Marx. While he did not agree with all the tenets of Marxist socialism, he did agree with many of them. What was Marxism? Nehru expressed his opinion about in a letter he wrote to his daughter from jail.

"It is a way of interpreting history, politics, economics, human life, and desires. It is a theory as well as a call to action. It is a philosophy which has something to say about most of the activities of man's life. It is an attempt at reducing human history, past, present, and future, to a rigid local system with something of the inevitability of fate or kismet about it. Whether life is so logical after all, and so dependent on hard and fast rules and systems, does not seem very obvious and many have doubted this. But Marx surveyed history as a scientist and drew certain conclusions from it. He saw from the earliest days man struggling for a living; it was a struggle against nature as well as against his brother-man."

Although Nehru called himself a socialist, he did not follow Marx all the way. Had he been an orthodox Marxist, he would have held that historic sequences could be not only followed analytically but also forecast by relating them to the modes of production, to economic causes. While Nehru agreed that economic factors did play important roles in history, he did not believe that knowledge of them enabled a person to act as a prophet. Man is too complicated a creature to respond only to one type of stimuli. The diversity of influences made it impossible to give valid predictions about the future.

Nehru had begun to write letters to Indira while he was in jail. She was alone most of the time, deprived of his guiding influence. Her mother could not provide an education; she was sickly and she lacked a basic education herself. The grandmother was old and also without schooling. One day it occurred to Nehru that he could give his daughter a "correspondence course." On her thirteenth birthday, in 1930, her father, again in jail, wished to give her a present. She had plenty of tangible gifts but she needed something else—her father's guiding spirit. He put it into a book, which became a classic.

"On your birthday you have been in the habit of receiving presents and good wishes," Nehru wrote her. "Good wishes you will still have in full measure, but what present can I give you from Naini prison? My presents cannot be very material or solid. They can only be of the air and of the mind and spirit, such as a good fairy might have bestowed on you—something that even the high walls of the prison cannot stop." Thus began a stream of letters which became the best present Indira ever received, *Glimpses of World History,* a sizable volume. Writing this book without research material was a great achievement, attesting to Nehru's remarkable grasp of history and to the sustained force of his willpower. When writing his world history, he also introduced his own recollections of contemporary events.

Here is a sample: "Early in the twentieth century an event occurred that had a great effect on the mind of Asia. This was the defeat of Tsarist Russia by Japan. . . . I remember well how excited I used to get when news came of the Japanese victories. I was about your age then."

This was the conclusion which Nehru reached in his letters to Indira:

"Our age . . . is an age of disillusion, of doubt, uncertainty and questioning. We can no longer accept many of the ancient beliefs and customs; we have no more faith in them, in Asia or in Europe or America. So we search for new ways. . . . Sometimes the injustice, the unhappiness, the brutality of the world oppress us and darken our minds, and we see no way out. . . . And yet if we take such a dismal view we have not learned aright the lesson of life or of history. For history teaches us of growth and of progress and of the possibility of an infinite advance for man."

The letter-writing from prison ended when Indira approached sixteen, in August, 1933. Jawaharlal felt elated to have hit upon this "remote-control" system of education.

His delight was expressed by the triumphant words he scribbled at the end of the last letter: *"Taman Shud."* The letters were written in English, but the parting expression was the Persian for "It is finished." (In India, Persian was once the language of the higher classes.)

Three weeks after the completion of the book, on August 30, 1933, Nehru, nearing forty-five, was released from Dehra Dun, and thus ended his sixth term of imprisonment. This time he was released, as previously, before the expiration of his term, and as on a previous occasion, his release was due to illness in the family. This time, his mother was ill. Nehru hurried to her bedside. His presence was a tonic and gradually her condition improved. However, Nehru's freedom was once again not to last long—five months and thirteen days.

Before that, parts of India were shaken by a tragedy. The day was January 15, 1934, and the midday hours in Allahabad were filled with sunshine. Nehru's car was waiting to take him to the railway station for a Congress meeting. He was about to go down the staircase when suddenly the earth began to shake, and tiles slid down the roof of the house. An earthquake, Nehru thought. It had been an earthquake, indeed, and a most tragic one. Some ten million people were rendered homeless over an area of thirty thousand square miles, and thousands of lives were lost. The center of the quake was east of Allahabad in the province of Bihar, an area of large population concentration.

Gandhi was at the meeting Nehru attended. His first words were, "Our punishment for committing the sin of untouchability."

Nehru's first words were, "What are the authorities doing to relieve the distress?"

The difference in the attitudes of the two men came to the fore again. Yet, they acted as one in offering aid.

Nehru's practical mind suggested, "Let's go into the afflicted area and help."

Promptly he organized the Allahabad Earthquake Relief Committee, and he himself moved into the hardest-hit area, the center of Bihar. One of his first visits was to the city of Monghyr, the historical walled-in center of medieval Muslim culture. While the inhabitants were mainly Muslims, the relief workers were mostly Hindus. This was one way of removing the barrier between the creeds.

Nehru and his fellow workers set to work. Government aid was not enough and so they launched a campaign to collect relief money from the rich estate-owners. But they soon ran into difficulty. "Yes," the magnates said, "help must come—God's own aid." They promised to pray at their favorite shrines.

In one village, the Nehru team entered one of the hamlets, which was completely destroyed; the mud huts were scattered on the powdery ground. The village inhabitants squatted along the trail from the highway and on the sites of their shattered huts. They were sunk in apathy, their idle hands by their sides. What could they do? their careworn faces seemed to say. The disaster was *malesh,* Allah's will. Or it was one of the forty crores of gods taking revenge for having been ignored. How was the ignorant peasant to know which of the four hundred million divinities was important?

Nehru, a scowl on his face, grabbed the nearest utensils and began to remove the debris. He told the peasants that not helping their neighbors and themselves was irreligious. He quoted well-known lines from the sacred writ of the

Bhagavad-Gita, to the effect that man was his own instrument of salvation and that the fight for life had no end.

Wherever Nehru and his small band of activists went, they stirred the populace into action. The little money they could distribute was less important than the energy they displayed. Nehru was recognized in many places, and word of his arrival in a village often preceded him on his swift trek. By the time he arrived, the villagers would be at work digging themselves out of the wreckage. People liked working with him because of his aura, that invisible, all-pervading blessing of a great man.

The earthquake-relief work taught Nehru many lessons. He learned that it was possible to mobilize the different creeds of India for a common cause. He also learned that leadership in India played an exceptionally important role. Above all, he learned that he had the capacity to take practical measures, to snap out of his brooding nature and to become a man of deeds.

∾ SEVEN ∾

A World Tragedy and a Trip Abroad

Now the world was convulsed by a political and economic earthquake. In the heart of Europe, proud of itself for its regard for the dignity of man, dark forces tried to destroy that pride. A preacher of hatred took over the government of Germany. He was Adolf Hitler, who set up a regime directed against all who disagreed with him. Even in France, the land of "enlightenment," the forces of darkness were bent on demolishing the country's democracy. Spain was soon to explode in a civil war. In the Far East, extreme militarists in Japan prepared for a Tokyo-controlled empire designed to encompass all of Asia. The United States was engulfed in an economic catastrophe that had thrown some fifteen million people out of work.

Nehru tried to relate these world events to developments in India. He found that while the rest of the world was going through momentous changes, India had fallen into the doldrums. People were getting tired of demonstrations, of being hustled to jail. They were even weary of civil disobedience, of satyagraha. The Great Soul of the national movement also showed signs of wear. He was concentrating his endeavors on working for the harijans. A worthy cause, to be sure, Nehru thought, but the core problem of India should not be overlooked—meaningful independence. Not just nominal independence, with a new crew of rulers, and business as usual. Freedom had to serve a practical purpose, too. In a country where millions died of starvation, freedom should mean food as well as free elections; the ability to acquire the skills to make two blades of grass grow where only one grew before; schools for all children. And, Nehru reflected sadly, Gandhi, Mr. India, the man whom he admired beyond all bounds, concerned himself with only one phase of the problem, instead of all phases. Nehru believed that a nationalist in India had to be a socialist, too, concerned with the entire social spectrum of life. He was a socialist; Gandhi was not.

Meanwhile, personal matters occupied Nehru's attention. Indira was now sixteen; a bright girl, somewhat introspective, moody, strong-willed, sometimes gay, but—like himself—inclined to sadness. She was lonely, too, as he had been, for her parents had little time for her. Kamala was still ailing, and Nehru himself spent his life in jails, at party meetings, on lecture tours, and traveling. There was little time for the young girl, and so he looked about for a guru for her.

One of Jawaharlal's heroes was India's great writer, Rabindranath Tagore, the Nobel Prize winner. A prolific author with an overabundance of energy, Tagore reminded Nehru of his own father, with his Olympian laughter and his belief in a full and joyous life. "The Poet"—as Gandhi called Tagore—loved children, and had founded a unique school, the famous Santiniketan at Bolpur, in Bihar, ninety miles from Calcutta. Later it developed into an international university, Visva-Bharati. He spent the Nobel Prize money for its upkeep. It was an open-air school in which the pupils remained in constant contact with nature, working in the gardens as well as in classrooms. It was a student-centered school, adjusted to the personal needs of the adolescent. Tagore had become acquainted with this type of institution on a visit to America. Nehru could find no better father-substitute for Indira than the Poet. So it was decided that the young girl should study in his school.

Another family event was the marriage of Nehru's younger sister, Krishna, to a lawyer from the province of Gujerat, Gandhi's home. The bridegroom, Raja Hutheesing, had an Oxford education, and that gave cause to some good-natured banter since Nehru was a Cambridge man. The wedding took place without much pomp in Allahabad.

The year of 1934 opened inauspiciously for the Indian independence movement. The British government was at work on a plan to appease the Congress party. Nehru had indications that little of what India expected would be granted in the British offer. He went around the country giving his views on what the future of India should be. It should be independent and socialist. The British were welcome to stay—as advisers, not as masters. India needed their technical skills but not their political rule. In due time, the British took notice of his views—with a vengeance.

On the afternoon of February 12, 1934, Nehru was having tea with Kamala on the veranda. Suddenly he had a premonition that the pleasant family interlude was to be interrupted. A minute later a car stopped in front of the Abode of Bliss, a well-known landmark to police cars by then. A young Britisher got out and approached Nehru with an apologetic smile. "The warrant is from Calcutta," he said in a tone indicating that he would have preferred to come on another errand.

"Yes," Nehru said with his sad smile. "I know the time is up."

By now Kamala was used to having family teas interrupted by the police. Quickly she went upstairs to prepare her husband's "jail bundle." However, this time she had a strange foreboding, and she took her time in collecting the bundle as if she wanted to prolong the moment of parting. Nehru noted Kamala's wistful look, and their parting was particularly painful. From the Abode of Bliss, Nehru was whisked to the Presidency Jail of Calcutta. He was tried and sentenced to two years for his anti-British speeches.

On previous occasions Nehru had been lodged in jails in pleasant locations, in view of snow-covered mountains, adjacent to hill stations or vacation spas. This time he was to have no view of the mountain peaks and no canopy of the highland sky over him. He remained in Calcutta and was lodged in its Alipore Central Jail.

Many people considered Calcutta the hellhole of creation. There the mass suffering of half-starved millions rubbed elbows with the ostentatious wealth of the few who ran the complex industrial, trading, and shipping empires of the metropolis. Calcutta was particularly hectic at that time, and the prison personnel reflected its short-tempered nature. In most of his previous jail homes, Nehru received "deluxe" treatment, for he was a famous man. But in Calcutta this was not so. A ten-by-nine cell was assigned to him, and he was kept locked up most of the day. He could not help comparing himself with a caged animal. Never before had he realized the dehumanization of being thrust into a cage. Why was he thus punished? Because he sympathized with fellow human beings and dared to express the "subversive" view that all men were created equal, even in India?

Luckily for Nehru, his periods of mental depression were short. He always found work for himself in jail—reading, writing to Indira as part of her education, or outlining his own autobiography. In the end, the autobiography turned out to be a political treatise containing little about his personal life and much about the movement and his relation to other Congress members, especially Gandhi.

More than ever he felt the need of exercise in his stiflingly hot cell. Now he made really good use of the Hindu yoga. His solitude stimulated intense concentration, the yoga essence. He could cast off trivial thoughts and focus his attention on ideas, ideals, and the mission of the individual to become a part of the community. He became adept in *pranayam,* the yoga breathing-exercise which links the breath with the soul. Also he practiced the *shirshasana,* standing on his head with interlocked fingers supporting the back of his head, elbows on the floor, his body upright. A ridiculous posture? He found it slightly funny at first. As his cerebral functions became stimulated, he found it animating, and his best thoughts occurred to him when standing on his head. He called these "spurts of illumination." He believed that this posture helped him to maintain his mental balance, since occasionally he showed a tendency to take himself too seriously. At such times all he had to do was to stand on his head and his pompousness was gone. He liked to say that he became really human upside-down.

Calcutta was hot and humid under the lid of the smoke-filled air, and in spite of the exercises, Nehru began to look weaker as deep shadows circled his clear eyes. Kamala, in town for medical treatment, was his frequent visitor in the Alipore Jail. He had the impression that she looked even frailer than before, the shadows deepening under her eyes, too. They worried about each other.

Then one day a prison official gave Nehru orders to be ready for transfer to another jail. This was May, the most try-ing month in tropical Calcutta, and so Nehru welcomed any change. He was taken to Dehra Dun, his old prison, and this pleased him.

He was now again in the highlands, where the clean air of the Himalayan peaks penetrated even into the convicts' cells. But Nehru's cell no longer faced the snow-covered giants in the distance. The prison walls were higher now so that much of his view was cut off. In spite of that, the in-vigorating scent of the mountain slopes wafted in on the northern winds. In this jail he regained much of the energy to carry out the plan that he had outlined in Alipore. It would be the story of his political life, a thought-cleansing process, a dialogue with the master, Mahatma Gandhi.

In the new prison the authorities were considerate of Nehru's health; in fact, his health had prompted the change of jails. They were even more considerate of Kamala's condition, which was deteriorating week by week. Then the prison warden told Nehru to get ready for another trip. This time he was allowed to go home, where Kamala was now very ill, and he was granted a suspension of his sentence, in order to be with her.

Kamala looked wan, more frail than ever, with the signs of her fatal ailment written on her hollow cheeks. Swaruprani, now in her mid-sixties and looking even older, seemed to be in poor health, too. Since Motilal's death, life had been very hard for her. She was worried about Kamala and about Jawaharlal, too. Young Indira was home for a visit from the Poet's school at Santiniketan. Now seventeen, she should have been full of life and fun, but in the saddened house she could not be happy. Perceptive beyond her age, she knew how gravely ill both her mother and grandmother were. And her father might again be committed to jail. It was not a gay family reunion.

Yet the days Nehru spent at home had a tonic effect on Kamala. She seemed to recover somewhat. The authorities allowed Nehru to be home only so long as his wife's life appeared to be in danger. Eleven days after his temporary release, the familiar police car called at the Nehru residence. Back to jail he went, but this time not to Dehra Dun. He was to stay closer to his family, and, therefore, he was taken to Naini. Again the authorities showed concern for the Nehrus. They would have released him altogether except that shortly the Congress party was holding its annual session in Bombay and they did not want him to be there; his presence would help make it a success—an eventuality the British wished to avoid. While in jail, Nehru received daily medical bulletins about the state of Kamala's health. Again she was deteriorating and a month later he was given another leave. He was shortly returned to jail, but he was given permission to visit his wife twice a week. Word was conveyed to him that he might be released if he gave his word to refrain from political action. Kamala heard of this and told him in a whisper, "Don't do it. Give no assurance to the government."

Allahabad, in the hot Ganges plains, was not the best place for a TB patient, and Kamala was moved to the fresher air of the mountain station at Bhowali. This time, the authorities transferred Nehru to Almora prison, on a Himalayan ridge, nearer to Bhowali, so that he could visit her.

Nehru was an expert on the prisons of India by now and he gave Almora a high rating. He had a large hall at his disposal, which he occupied in the company of some forty fellow inmates—sparrows. So again he was close to nature. Mountains filled his horizon. He saw them as the primeval efforts of the earth to reach for the infinite. By family tradition, he was a mountain man, being of Kashmiri stock, even though he was born in the Ganges lowlands. His own life cycle seemed to be influenced by the mountains; like them, he was striving toward the infinite, attempting to soar. But how could he soar across the prison walls? Looking at the landscape, he felt a creative elation that impelled him to jot down his thoughts with great haste. Thus, he continued to write his *Glimpses of World History,* which contained more Nehru than the historic characters he portrayed. He also wrote his autobiography.

Politics dominated the interest of India once more. At long last the British came forth with their plan of loosening their hold on the peninsula. The plan was the work of the

Simon commission, in part, but, by and large, it was the work of the Congress party. The proposal called for extension of limited civic rights to the people of India, who were to have an elected Central Federal Assembly. But it was so constituted as to represent diverse communities: Hindus, Muslims, the princes, and the many minorities. The governments of the provinces under this arrangement, on the other hand, were to be more expressive of the Indians' will. To Nehru, the plan still seemed to be a roundabout way of maintaining Britain's hold. The complicated structure was to facilitate the old imperialist game of divide and rule. Nehru and his associates wanted immediate independence, and this was not it.

The British offer was sad news for Nehru in jail. No less sad was the news that his wife had again taken a turn for the worse. Now the physicians recommended that she be taken to a hill resort for tuberculous patients, the Badenweiler Sanatorium in the Black Forest region of Germany. Quickly, preparations were made, and soon Kamala was on her way, accompanied by Indira, who had to leave school. Nehru had been given leave from jail to see his wife off. It was a sad departure, witnessed also by Swaruprani and Krishna.

After Kamala's departure, Nehru had to return to his prison home, this time again in Almora. No longer was he enchanted by the twittering company of his friends the birds. Uncertain about Kamala's fate, he was deeply depressed.

Kamala's doctor sent regular bulletins, which reached not only Nehru in his jail cell, but also the British authorities in Allahabad and, probably, in New Delhi. Otherwise, how could one explain their concern for the plight of the family? Nehru still had about six months of his term to serve, but he was released from jail, and the authorities indicated that he was free to visit his wife abroad. The superintendent escorted him to the prison gate on September 4, 1935. The Indian leader was now almost forty-six years old.

The following day he was on a plane, headed for Europe, where he met Indira. Nehru liked to be with her, an intelligent young woman, now eighteen, with whom he could talk about many things, including politics. His letters from prison had brought him closer to his daughter. She was no longer to be neglected. The plane ride from India to Europe took several days in that era. As soon as Nehru landed in Europe, he rushed to Kamala's bedside.

She was not cheerful and her features looked drawn. But she brightened up quickly with her family near her. Spending much of his time in the sickroom, Nehru was again assailed by remorse. Had he done his share to make Kamala happy at home? He had had so little time to spend with her, and now he accused himself of neglect. Why had he been guilty of neglecting his wife? Because he was always concerned with what he considered his larger family—the people of India. Would it not have been better even for India if he had concentrated his attention on his wife and child? What would happen if everyone concerned oneself with the welfare of the whole while neglecting the part? Probably it would be better if people concerned themselves with the tiny worlds of their own, the world they knew best, which, after all, formed part of the larger world. His lack of deeper concern may have been one cause of Kamala's physical ailment. Carried away by pangs of conscience, Nehru now spent his time in the company of his wife.

While Kamala was happy in his company, Nehru could

not help but notice that prolonged visits sapped too much of her strength. There could be no doubt that, in spite of her brave front, the condition of his wife was worsening. It seemed to the attending physicians that the visits should be stopped. It was decided that he and Indira should go to England.

Politics, as well as the advice of Kamala's doctors, took Nehru back to England. He had a manuscript that he wanted to publish in Britain and other parts of the English-speaking world. "This book was written entirely in prison," he wrote in the preface. "The primary object in writing these pages was to occupy myself with a definite task. . . . My attempt was to trace, as far as I could, my own mental development, and not to write a survey of recent Indian history." Eventually, it was published under the title *Jawaharlal Nehru: An Autobiography.*

For Nehru, Britain was like a homecoming. He met some of his former schoolmates, who were very much aware of his fame. They teased him for his attempts to undermine the British Empire, which so many of the distinguished alumni from his alma maters had helped to strengthen.

While in London, Nehru established close contact with a man who was to play a significant role in Indian history. His name was Krishna Menon. With his exotic, saturnine looks, Menon was handsome in a diabolic way. He came from the Malabar Coast in southern India. He had established a small office of the India League in the heart of London, which he had turned into a high-pressure public relations headquarters, a lobby of Indian independence. In performing his work, Menon established close contacts with some of Britain's leading politicians, especially with members of the Labour party, whose views he shared. His India League published pamphlets, organized lectures, and sought to hold together the Indian community in the British capital. Krishna Menon felt affinity for Nehru's political views, and created a lobby for him, too. The two men were to play important roles in each other's lives. Both were intellectuals, different from the rank and file of the National Congress party bigwigs, who had few intellectual aspirations and were mainly party politicians. It was easy for Nehru and Menon to find subjects of common interest. Sitting in his office, close to a stove, a heavy shawl around his neck even in the summer, drinking countless cups of dark tea, Menon introduced Nehru to the latest developments of Britain's political life. England was passing through a difficult period of its history. Unemployment was chronic and too high for the size of the country. It was believed by very many Britishers that conditions would deteriorate further if the empire were to lose India. Menon disagreed with this view. He maintained that Britain would gain both prestige and economic substance if India were to become a free member of the British Commonwealth. He sought to give this direction to the thinking of British politicians, and his power of persuasion was strong. Nehru, naturally, agreed with him.

The two men also agreed on other important issues. Both believed that India, when freed, should look to the future. The present was the capitalism of Britain and America. Conditions in those countries were different from India. Britain and America had capital and so they could afford capitalism. India had little capital, and, therefore, capitalism was not for her. She would have to combine all her social resources under a socialist economy. Nehru and Menon considered socialism the system of the future.

Krishna Menon introduced Nehru to leading members of

the British Labour party, who were to play significant roles in
history, and he organized lectures for him in the India
League. Through Menon, Nehru met publishers, who showed
interest in the Indian leader's books. It was a fruitful trip
and one which diverted Nehru's mind from Kamala's health.
He was also able to spend a great deal of time with Indira.

Nehru was in London when a great honor was conferred
on him in India. He was reelected president of the National
Congress party for 1936-37. Gandhi was his main sponsor,
in spite of their disagreements on important issues. The
Great Soul exhibited his true greatness by promoting the
presidential candidacy of the "impatient young man" who
wanted to speed up the course of history; unlike the "impatient young man," Gandhi believed that history's forces
followed their own laws.

After twelve days, the London trip had to be broken off.
Nehru was called back to Kamala's bedside. She rallied after
his return, and then once again had a relapse. Her condition
was aggravated by the death of a fellow patient to whom
she had become devoted. At her request, she was taken to
a Swiss sanatorium in Leysin, near Lausanne, which was reported to have a highly competent medical staff.

The Nehrus found Leysin singularly attractive. It was a
beautiful spot perched high on a mountain slope, enwrapped
in the purest Alpine air. Kamala, resting on a balcony of the
sanatorium, was surrounded by an enchanting scene. At the
foot of the mountains, a short distance away, she saw Lake
Geneva, with its azure waves cleft by swiftly moving, snow-
white boats. She never tired of looking at the massive peak
Dent du Midi (Tooth of the South), projecting its vastness
into the sky. Kamala feasted her eyes on nature's dramatic
show each day.

Nehru wanted to stay with her, but she insisted that, having been elected Congress president, he must attend to his duties in India. He was about to leave when he received a call from Kamala's physician who had just completed an examination of his patient. He strongly advised Nehru to postpone his departure. Therefore, both husband and daughter were at Kamala's bedside when she died on February 28, 1936.

According to Hindu custom, Kamala's body was cremated and the ashes placed in an urn which Nehru took with him. The nearest airport was a short distance away, in Montreux. From there, Nehru wired the dedication of his book to his British publisher: "To Kamala, Who Is No More."

Nehru was now internationally famous, and news of his stay in Switzerland had became known. Word was conveyed to him at the airport that an Italian diplomat requested the honor of being presented to him. The diplomat brought the sympathy of the Italian government head, Benito Mussolini. Then the diplomat told Nehru of Mussolini's request. Since Nehru's plane made a scheduled stop in Rome, the Italian leader asked that the two men get together for a talk.

Nehru—a courteous man—would, under other circumstances, have had no objection to this interruption of his homeward journey. But his wife had just died. And besides, Mussolini was not merely a government head. His country had just recently crushed Ethiopia, hitherto the only free East African nation. Now Italy was set to absorb the small country into its overseas empire. Nehru was a democrat and a socialist; Mussolini was opposed to democracy and was a Fascist, an enemy of socialism. Nehru excused himself. He was not going to call on the Italian ruler.

The affair was not closed, however. As scheduled, the

plane made a stopover in the Italian capital. At the airport Nehru had another caller, no less courteous than the first, but more insistent. He was Mussolini's own *chef de cabinet,* chief of his private office, and he not only repeated the previous invitation but also added his own personal plea. It was most important for the chief personally to arrange this interview, as his job might depend on the success of his mission. But Nehru felt that a principle was at stake, and so he stood his ground. His principles were more important than his desire to heed a personal plea.

Homeward bound, Nehru speculated about the insistence of the Italian dictator. Several thoughts occurred to him. In connection with the rape of Ethiopia, Mussolini was waging a diplomatic cold war against Britain. Nehru's homeland was doing the same for the sake of its independence. Yet, Nehru saw that the two wars were basically different. Mussolini had crushed a people; the Indian Congress party wanted to revive one. By accepting the invitation of the Fascist leader, Nehru might have conveyed the impression that he considered Mussolini a fellow fighter in a righteous cause.

In a few days, Nehru was back again in his homeland. From one house of sorrow, the Swiss sanatorium where his wife died, he moved now into another house of grief, his own home. His mother had been the victim of two paralytic strokes, and it was clear to her son that she would not live much longer. Yet, even though her health was failing, she followed political events and was the proudest of mothers to see the joy that the return of her son engendered all over India. She was also proud of the fact that he was again head of the fighting arm of the Indian independence movement, the National Congress party.

As Congress president, Nehru could not stay long at home. His mother wanted him to throw himself into his work with all his energy. And he did. As president of the party at a crucial period in Indian history, he was in a key position to take decisive steps.

We have seen that as a result of the recommendations of the Simon commission, the British government offered India a measure of participation in the conduct of its affairs. But it was a restricted participation. Implementation of the recommendations would have perpetuated the immensely complicated and self-defeating organization of the past—the crazy quilt of sects, classes, castes, languages, and interlocking princely rules. Consequently, Nehru and the Congress party rejected the part of the British plan referring to all-Indian federal affairs. However, the plan that the British government proposed for the provinces seemed to be more equitable. India consisted of a number of provinces, corresponding to the American states, and, in many instances, with larger populations. At any rate, it was to the advantage of the Indian freedom movement to acquire training grounds for administrators and legislators. So the Congress party accepted the plan relating to home rule in the provinces. Elections followed and in many of them the Congress party took control.

This was now a constructive period, uninterrupted by terms in jail. Nehru was very much in the center of events. All the world knew that he was the crown prince of the frail little man in the loincloth, the Great Soul.

In the midst of this whirlwind of activity, Nehru's mother had a third stroke in 1938 and died, surrounded by her children.

Shortly after her death, Nehru received an invitation to visit Germany, then under Nazi rule. The chancellor of the Third Reich, Adolf Hitler, glorified an extreme form of nationalism, a crude economic equalitarianism, martial virtues, and the "purity of blood." "Aryan" was the term he applied to "racial purity"—of the Indo-European type. He may have wanted to see Nehru in order to establish closer links between the bearers of the original name of Aryan—the Indians—and the "new Aryan"—the Germans. But Nehru was not disposed to enter into such discussions. However, the invitation to Berlin aroused his latent wanderlust. He decided to go—not to Germany—but to his intellectual home, Britain, and also to Spain.

Nehru flew to Britain, where his daughter was taking courses at the Somerville College of Oxford. Indira was also engaged in political work. She was a member of the Majlis, the organization of Indian students in England, and was in contact with Krishna Menon.

This time, therefore, it was a father-daughter team that called on Menon. Nehru wanted to enlist Menon's aid in arranging publication of two more books that he had written. One of them was *Glimpses of World History,* largely the course he had conducted in jail for the benefit of his daughter.

Nehru also renewed his friendships with British political leaders, members of the Labour party. He found much understanding—even more than on his last visit—for the problems of India. It seemed to many Labourites that the political situation, in regard to Britain and all her possessions, was assuming two clear-cut sides: the Right, which believed that its culture should be the culture of all British posses-

sions; and the Left, which believed that each colony had the
right to live according to its own ideas. British colonial supremacy was incompatible with the Left view.

Leaving Indira at Somerville for a while, Nehru, accompanied by Menon, traveled to Spain. It was June, 1938, and
the air was velvety, the sky serene. But the countryside was
not serene, because there was murder in the Spaniards' eyes;
they were slaughtering one another in a massive civil war.
Again it was a conflict between the Right and the Left. The
Right was headed by General Francisco Franco, and the
Left by a coalition government, including a broad spectrum,
from the liberals to the Communists. The visitors from India
saw the Left as the expression of the people's aspiration to
make their country safe for the common man.

At the time of their visit, the Spanish government was
on the defensive. "I saw much," Nehru wrote in Barcelona,
the provisional capital of the government, "that impressed
me powerfully; and there in the midst of want and destruc-
tion and ever-impending disaster I felt more at peace with
myself than anywhere else in Europe. There was light there,
the light of determination and of doing something worth-
while."

The two visitors called on key figures in the region controlled by the government. One of these was "General
Lister," a former stonemason—his real name unknown to
them—who commanded an important fighting sector. Lister
gave an excellent account of himself, and the visiting
Indians thought this provided a lesson which they might
be able to apply at home. The lesson was that top military
gifts were not necessarily the products of top military men in
India, whose main asset seemed to be an inflated sense of

dignity. "Alas for this old type," Nehru noted, "which shines so much at polo, bridge, and on the parade-grounds. . . ."

The two men from India also met a remarkable woman, the middle-aged daughter of a Basque miner and the mother of several grown children. She knew how to keep the flames of enthusiasm alive, and she spoke to the visitors "fiercely and ardently in a torrent of lilting Spanish." Because of her passionate involvement in the people's cause, the world came to know her as La Pasionaria—the Passionflower.

Nehru and Menon met, among others, Alvarez del Vayo, a former journalist and now foreign minister of the embattled Spanish Republic. He was an effective diplomat, from whom they learned another significant lesson. Professional diplomats had no monopoly on the knowledge of foreign affairs. The independent India the two men envisaged would be able to succeed with the aid of nonprofessional diplomats of the Alvarez del Vayo type; people fired by dreams and tempered by common sense.

Back in England, Nehru picked up Indira, while Menon stayed in London, keeping the India League lobby in high gear. The Nehrus paid a quick visit to Prague, the capital of Czechoslovakia. The Republic of Czechoslovakia was the first country on Hitler's timetable of conquest. Nehru saw that the Czechs, a democratic people, would not be able successfully to oppose Nazi aggression.

Six months had elapsed since Nehru had left India, and now he had to return home. He left Europe with a heavy heart. He saw the darkening of the horizon, the arrogance of aggressive nations, the meekness of the forces of peace. He could not foresee, nor could anyone else, the tragedy which was to overwhelm the old and seemingly tired continent. Shortly after Nehru's visit in Spain, the republican government was crushed and the Fascist forces triumphed.

Again in India, Nehru saw little progress. The Congress party controlled the government in six provinces—Bihar, Bombay, Madras, the Central Provinces, Orissa, and the United Provinces; two more, the Frontier Province and Assam, were to come under its rule later. But these provincial governments could not do too much to introduce major reforms. The princely states, mostly conservative, were still ruled by the British.

Although the British still held India, Nehru and his associates realized that freedom must come soon. Therefore, plans would have to be made for the future. They visualized one India, occupying the entire subcontinent. It was a unit; nature had made it so by surrounding it with natural frontiers, the highest mountains in the world in the north, and oceans bordering the rest of the country. India was also an economic unit. But to this one-India plan a new obstacle arose in the person of Mohammed Ali Jinnah, head of the Muslim League.

The Congress party claimed to represent all the people of India, irrespective of religion—Hindus, Muslims, Parsees, Jains, Buddhists, Christians, and others. The Muslim League, on the other hand, claimed to speak for the people who followed Islam. What were the aspirations of the league and who was Jinnah, its leader?

The word *Jinnah* means "the lean one," and lean he was indeed: a tall man with a pinched, austere face. "If the British leave the subcontinent," he said, "there must be two countries; one for the Hindus and the other one for the

Muslims." And he added, "This is because Hindus and Muslims are two different breeds of people."

Nehru replied that this was the wrong approach. The people of India had common interests despite their different backgrounds. In a free India, they would do best by working together for the common cause—raising the tragically low living standard.

In the midst of this argument, the world was engulfed in flames.

～ EIGHT ～

Then Came Another World War

Hitler's Germany crushed Czechoslovakia. A year later, in the late summer of 1939, Hitler moved against Poland. Britain and France were bound by pacts to come to the aid of the Poles. Thus, World War II began. Eventually, two other major countries joined the Germans—Italy and Japan. The three powers came to be known as the Berlin-Rome-Tokyo Axis, or Axis, for short.

The British declared war on Germany, and they did this also in India's name. They did not, however, consult with Indian leaders about this, and the Indians resented the omission. Nehru and other Indians were against the Axis, and sympathized with Britain and France. But they deeply resented the fact that the British had not asked their approval for the declaration of war.

One of the Indian leaders, Subhas Chandra Bose, a former president of the Congress party, sneaked out of India, and joined forces with the Axis. The other leaders, although they disapproved of his action, reminded the British that if Indian public opinion was solidly behind them it would be of help to them in the war.

One of the first results of the British slur against the Indians was the resignation of the Congress party cabinets in the eight provinces of India. Within the party there were disagreements over the path to national freedom, but there was agreement about the ultimate aim. All the leaders wanted an independent India. Nehru advocated helping the British against the Fascist powers by any means, including war. He did this because he saw the Fascists as reactionary forces seeking to maintain the old order of arrogant ruling classes while pretending to represent the interests of the common man. Gandhi, however, took a different view. While he, too, wanted the Fascists defeated, he thought that this could best be accomplished by an ideological weapon. "I want you to fight Nazism without arms," he wrote in an "Appeal to Every Briton," which he made on July 6, 1940. "I claim to have been a lifelong and disinterested friend of the British people. . . . Whatever the ultimate fate of my country, my love for you remains, and will remain undiminished. My nonviolence demands universal love. . . . It is my love which has prompted my appeal to you."

That love did not animate the British, who knew that the Axis would never respond to it. This was another of those occasions when Nehru took issue with Gandhi.

"He does not know the dictator's mentality," Nehru commented. "Nor does he know that the world is governed by violence now, not satyagraha. If you oppose aggression with affection, you open the floodgates to a tidal wave."

Germany's quick moves had stunned the world. Hitler wiped independent Poland off the map in a matter of days. In the spring of 1940, he turned west, conquered Belgium, Holland, Denmark, and Norway, and overwhelmed French resistance. So mighty were his armed forces that there seemed to be no power to halt their march. The British had lost their foothold on the continent, and the Nazis were ready to launch Operation Sea Lion—the invasion of England. Preliminary to it, the German Luftwaffe, the air force, began the final attack to soften British resistance. However, it proved far from a final attack, and British resistance remained unbroken.

Yet, the danger to Britain was not over. During the lull, India took its stand. The Congress leaders wanted their price for aiding Britain. The price was independence, demanded in the Bombay Resolution, passed in the summer of 1940. It called upon the people not to cooperate actively with the British war effort until the country's claims were satisfied. It did not call for a concerted campaign of nonviolence, but did call for individual satyagraha as a protest. The first man to announce his noncooperation with the British was an associate of Gandhi's, Vinoba Bhave, who was to make a name for himself in years to come. He was arrested and sentenced to three months in prison.

Whenever a satyagraha campaign was launched, the British countered it with a routine procedure. They set up detention pens all over the country—jails, forts, or large sheds surrounded by walls—then rounded up the patriots, who usually had their small bundles ready to give them a minimum of comfort in jail. To the patriots, it was a badge of honor to be crammed into police wagons.

By now arrest and jailing were routine for Nehru. He felt as much at home in jail as in the Abode of Bliss. This time he was arrested at a railway station on his return from Wardha, Gandhi's place of retreat. The detention warrant specified the charge against him. He had spoken for non-violent noncooperation with the British. Again he was tried in jail—a procedure that saved transportation costs. This time it was in Gorakhpur, a historic place close to the site said to be the Buddha's burial place. Nehru's defense before the Gorakhpur magistrate became a classic of India's political literature. He placed his accusers on the defensive and expressed the national aspirations of India.

"I stand before you, sir," he said in a clear and ringing voice, "as an individual being tried for certain offenses against the state. You are a symbol of that state. But I am something more than an individual also; I, too, am a symbol at the present moment, a symbol of Indian nationalism, resolved to break away from the British Empire and achieve the independence of India. It is not me that you are seeking to judge and condemn, but rather the hundreds of millions of the people of India. . . . Perhaps it may be thought, that I am standing before you on my trial; it is the British Empire itself that is on trial before the bar of the world. . . . It is a small matter to me what happens to me in this trial or subsequently. Individuals count for little; they come and go, as I shall go when my time is up. Seven times I have been tried and convicted by the British authority in India, and many years of my life lie buried within prison walls. An eighth time or a ninth, and a few more years, make little difference.

"But it is no small matter what happens to India and her millions of sons and daughters. That is the issue before me, and that ultimately is the issue before you, sir. If the British government imagines it can continue to exploit them and play about with them against their will, as it has done for so long in the past, it is grievously mistaken. It has misjudged their present temper and read history in vain.

"I should like to add that I am happy to be tried in Gorakhpur. The peasantry of Gorakhpur are the poorest and the most long-suffering in my province. I am glad that it was my visits to Gorakhpur and my attempt to serve its people that has led to this trial."

The court sentenced Nehru to four years in jail.

During the time he was in jail, the German armies staged their spectacular victories. After they had overrun France, they marched into Yugoslavia. The Yugoslavs held out longer than the French had, but in the end, they too were crushed. Then war spread to the Mediterranean, as Hitler's Italian allies moved into Greece. Subsequently, North Africa, too, became a theater of war. After the Italians suffered initial defeats, the Germans swept into the region, duplicating their European victories. Then on June 22, 1941, Hitler struck at the Soviet Union.

The Nazi armies scored spectacular successes there, too, at first. German radio announcements usually began with martial strains proclaiming the capture of Russian cities. No force on earth seemed to equal Nazi might. The German armies smashed across the steppes of that vast country. Moscow held out, but the Germans penetrated deep into the interior, and headed for the Volga River, the Soviet lifeline.

Nehru read about these events in jail and he recorded in his recollections: "We followed with anxious interest the dramatic changes in the war situation."

He also followed with anxious interest another dramatic event, far from the theaters of war, on the other side of the Atlantic.

In the United States, President Franklin D. Roosevelt with Winston Churchill, prime minister of Great Britain, drew up a historic document, the Atlantic Charter, in August, 1941. One of its eight points stipulated that all people should have the right to choose their own forms of government. India's four hundred million people certainly qualified to declare their own choice of government under the charter.

"Words," Nehru reflected, "words which are contradicted by the facts. The deception of world public opinion seems to have no bounds."

Nehru's eighth spell in prison terminated abruptly on December 4, 1941. Evidently, the British government had plans about India. Three days later Japan struck at Pearl Harbor in the Pacific, where a great part of the United States Navy was stationed. The object was to inflict a mortal wound on America. The Japanese warlords considered the United States their enemy because it sought to restrain Tokyo's aggressive policies. The United States entered World War II, and the most dramatic phase of the conflict now began.

The Japanese launched their attack along the huge arc of Southeast Asia. Singapore, the main naval base of the British, fell to them. In an incredible burst of energy, Japan took the three thousand emerald islands of the Netherlands East Indies. They did not need to take all these islands, of course, only the key ones, including Java, with about half of the colony's population; Borneo; Sumatra; and New Guinea, largest of the group.

With a swiftness that stunned the world, the Japanese then burst into Burma, India's neighbor, and ascended the heights separating these two parts of the British Empire. At the rate the conquering armies were going it seemed possible that they would sweep into India with the same irresistible force.

While the Japanese were thrusting westward, the Nazis were forging eastward. They smashed their way into Egypt, which was in British hands, although both its king and its government were friendly to the Nazis. Then they headed toward Egypt's jugular vein, the Suez Canal. If they could gain control of the canal, the main transportation artery of the Allies would be severed. From the canal, the Nazis planned to thrust toward the great oil areas of the Middle East. The Axis powers needed oil above all for their air forces.

Should they get the wells, they would be in an almost unbeatable position. This then was the situation: the Japanese were sweeping westward; the Germans, eastward. Their junction would mean their victory.

Meanwhile, Bose, the renegade Congress party leader, was calling upon his countrymen to utilize the golden opportunity of their freedom fight. The Japanese were set to descend from the border hills into the Indian heartland. With the aid of Indians living outside of the country, Bose had organized an Indian National Army, subject to the commands of a Free India government headed by him. His battle cry to his army was *Delhi Chalo*—"Onward to Delhi." Two Axis armies pressing for a junction and an India in revolt against the British would surely have spelled victory for Berlin and Tokyo.

During these troubled times, Nehru and his co-workers had a friend in the White House. President Roosevelt realized how strategic India's location was and how vulnerable she was to subversion. Through his personal envoys, he kept the situation under constant observation. His influence on events in the subcontinent is still not adequately known, but it may be assumed that he was pressing Britain to deal with the Congress party.

Early in 1942, the British government decided to face the problem of India. England's fortune was at its lowest. The government, headed by Winston Churchill, took a bold step. It dispatched a member of the government, Sir Stafford Cripps, to New Delhi with an offer of dominion status after the war. India was to remain linked to the United Kingdom and other dominions "by a common allegiance to the crown but equal to them in every respect, in no way subordinate in any aspect of its domestic and external affairs."

India's status was to be similar to that of Canada, and that meant complete independence within the empire. But— there again was that eternal "but"—all of these changes were to take place *after* the war. Why then and not now? There was also still the problem of the Lean One, with his Muslim League and its claims, and the hundreds of princes with their claims and treaty rights vouchsafed by the British. Nehru, Gandhi, and others saw this as another British exercise in prevarication. Nehru liked the British and trusted their fairness in their own domestic affairs. But in foreign affairs the British had a different face. The Cripps mission was a failure. Sir Stafford arrived in New Delhi on March 22, and was on his way back to London on April 11.

The failure of the Cripps mission caused new turmoil within the Congress party. What was to be done? Wait for another offer? How long? It was decided not to wait but to take action. No longer would the party petition the British—it would tell them what to do. They were to leave India. This demand was embodied in what is known as the Quit India Resolution.

Nehru specified one of the main complaints of the Congress party—the British plan for the princely states. "We strongly condemn the provisions of the British proposals that the rulers of the Indian states should nominate their representatives to the Constituent Assembly, thus ignoring the rights of the populations themselves." In spite of all of this, Nehru did not want to embarrass the British war effort in India. He subscribed to the view of his associate, Krishna Menon, who called upon the Churchill government: "Reconsider your stand; it is not too late. Release the political prisoners and end repression. Relieve the famine. Withdraw the ban on Congress. Recognize India's national independence!"

Meanwhile, an important event occurred in the Nehrus' family life. Indira fell in love with Feroze Gandhi, no relation to the Great Soul.

They had first met in Allahabad, about the time Indira was getting ready to go to England to continue her studies. Feroze was intelligent, strong-willed, self-assured, and handsome. Lacking the funds to join Indira in England, he induced a wealthy aunt to finance his trip. There he attended the London School of Economics, majoring in journalism and seeing a good deal of Indira. When he proposed to her, she wrote to her father, asking for his consent.

But even before that, Nehru had received word about the romance. People had written to him and they were deeply upset. Their indignation was aroused by the fact that Feroze was a Parsi, not a Hindu. He belonged to the small religious sect that followed the teachings of Zoroaster.

Differences in creed meant little to Nehru, but he was the leading person in the new India, and many of his followers were concerned about his daughter marrying a non-Hindu. Nehru was only concerned because Indira was everything to him and he did not want her to act impulsively. He was in jail when he received her letter, and he decided upon a strategy of delay.

Nehru wrote back to Indira, saying that she should take time to think the matter over. At any rate, she should wait until her father was freed. Nehru had been sentenced to a long spell in jail.

Unexpectedly, an amnesty was declared long before the expiration of Nehru's term. Indira had not changed her mind. So, in spite of the many protests, he gave his consent. Now a day had to be set for the wedding. The family astronomer was consulted and March 26, 1942, was chosen. It was the birthday of the hero of the epic poem *Ramayana*.

This is how Indira's aunt recalls her on her wedding day:

"Indira had never looked more lovely as she waited in her shell-pink sari, embroidered with silver and made of the finest khadi, spun by her father in jail. She was tall and rather frail, ethereal-looking, with very black hair that fell to her shoulders. She had large, dark eyes in an aquiline face, and a complexion the golden color of ripe wheat. In profile, Indira looked like the head on a Greek coin."

Surrounded by friends and relatives, the bride waited in her chambers for the "call." The auspicious moment—foretold by the astronomer—arrived. A marble platform had been erected on the lawn of Anand Bhawan for the ceremony, and the traditional fire had been kindled on its slabs. While the priests were tending the sacred flames, a canopy of brocade, supported by tall poles, was set upon the platform.

Nehru called for his daughter and escorted her to the platform where they took seats next to each other. At the climax of the ceremonial rites, Indira rose and went to the other side of the platform, where Feroze was sitting. While the priests fed the flames with ghee—the symbolic clarified butter—the young couple took the "seven steps," walking around the fire seven times while exchanging the marriage vows.

"May you live," the priests chanted, "as the God Shiva did with his spouse, Parvati, and the Lord Krishna with his wife, Radha. . . ." The young people took food from each other's hands—they were husband and wife now.

After their honeymoon in Kashmir, Indira and Feroze returned to Allahabad where they bought a small home. Unfortunately, they could not afford to enjoy married life there for long.

All the Nehrus were ardent fighters for the freedom of India. This was the time to press for it—while the Allies were fighting for a "free world" in the greatest war in history. Father Nehru was the first to be picked up and sent to Ahmednagar Fort, some two hundred miles from Bombay. With the father gone, the children continued the fight for India's freedom through the Congress party. Less than half a year after their wedding, Indira and Feroze were picked up by the British police and placed in Naini jail, close to home. There they joined other members of the Nehru family. It was in jail that Indira's twenty-fifth birthday was celebrated.

While the Nehrus were in jail, the tide of war turned completely, and the Allies took the offensive. Soon the Fascist powers were to be crushed. Soon India's fate had to be decided. In preparation for that decision, some of the Nehrus were freed.

Eventually, Feroze and Indira had two sons, Rajiv, meaning "lotus," in memory of Kamala, and Sanjay, after a character in the Bhagavad-Gita.

Feroze continued to work for India as a newspaper correspondent, editor, and publisher. He also became a member of parliament. Indira, meanwhile, was often needed at the prime minister's resident, as her father's official hostess. The rumor spread that she and Feroze were not on the best of terms.

Both were strong-willed and self-assured, and their marriage had many strains. A great problem was Feroze's health. He had had several serious heart attacks. Years later, he died in a nursing home, on September 8, 1960.

After Indira's marriage, Nehru had been lonely for a while. He went to the town of Kulu at an altitude of nine thousand feet. Mountains always had a salutary effect on him. "They make me want to sing," he used to say. "Only songs can express the highest degree of elation." In this mountain country he had the dramatic variety that the craggy landscape produced—gorges, cliffs, cataracts, and forests of deodar clothing the lower reaches of the slopes and towering above tiers of pine on rocky ledges. The exotic culture of the region attracted Nehru. Pockets of the area preserved ancient customs of polyandry, the system of multiple marriage in which one wife has several husbands. In general, there were in this region many similarities with the mores of parts of Tibet.

After a short stay at Kulu, Nehru returned to Allahabad. Through the grapevine he first heard about a new wave of

arrests of Congress leaders in the wake of the Quit India
Resolution, to which the British, naturally, objected. On an
early August day he saw the familiar sight of a police car
stopping in front of the Abode of Bliss with its police official,
with his embarrassed smile, and those customary papers of
detention.

The arrest procedure was familiar but the jail was not.
This time it was Ahmednegar Fort, a sixteenth-century edifice
about two hundred miles from Bombay. Feroze Gandhi,
Indira's husband, was arrested, too.

Indira did not want to be left alone. She led a parade of
women demonstrators marching down the main streets of
Allahabad, carrying placards addressed to the British: "Quit
India!" She was arrested and sentenced to thirteen months in
jail. The Nehru family lived up to their reputation as jailbirds in the cause of Indian freedom. In prison Indira plunged
into her work of teaching illiterate women how to read. She
had ample time for her work.

The Ahmednagar Fort contained almost the entire working
committee of the Congress party. Nehru's fellow prisoners
included Vallabhbhai Patel, considered the number-three man
in the movement, and Maulana Abul Kalam Azad, several
times president of the Congress party. He was not a Hindu
but a practicing Muslim, born in Mecca, Arabia, and a living
testimony to Gandhi's contention that their party expressed
the aspirations of all India, irrespective of creed. Other
prisoners in the jail were men who were to play important
roles in Indian history.

Life in the fort certainly was not boring; the diversity of
character traits and skills of the prisoners was large. Abul
Kalam Azad had the reputation of being a walking en-
cyclopedia. Acharya Kripalani, another prominent political,

was called a spirit of negation. Patel was the most practical-minded member of the group.

In Ahmednagar, Nehru wrote *The Discovery of India,* a classic. "This book was written by me," Nehru said in the preface, "in Ahmednagar Fort prison during the five months, April to September, 1944." It was an achievement that placed its author among the great historians of the century. He wrote:

> The new moon, a shimmering crescent in the darkening sky, greeted us on our arrival here. The bright fortnight of the waxing moon had begun. Ever since then each coming of the new moon has been a reminder to me that another month of my imprisonment is over. . . .

Then the sense of isolation:

> Three weeks we spent here cut off completely from all news of the outside world. There were no contacts of any kind, no interviews, no letters, no newspapers, no radio. Even our presence here was supposed to be a state secret unknown to any except officials in charge of us, a poor secret, for all India knew where we were. . . .

Then newspapers were allowed and with them knowledge of the chronic tragedy of India:

> Famine came, ghastly, staggering, horrible beyond words. In Malabar, in Bijapur, in Orissa, and above all

in the rich and fertile province of Bengal, men and women and little children died in the thousands daily for lack of food. They dropped down dead before the palaces of Calcutta, their corpses lay in the mud huts of Bengal's innumerable villages and covered the roads and fields of its rural areas. . . .

Thus began Nehru's discovery of India, mostly flashbacks, beginning with the story of ancient civilizations, and ending with the nationalist movement. It was no coincidence that first Nehru had written *Glimpses of World History,* preparatory to his *Discovery of India.* It required all these years to make that discovery because India was more complex than all the rest of the world. It had a million faces. And in discovering India, Nehru found himself—his enhanced sympathy for the underdog, which he expressed in one word, socialism.

Meanwhile, great changes were taking place on the battle-fronts. The Nazis and the Japanese, who had appeared to be invincible in 1942, were headed toward disaster a year later. German armor was blunted in Russia at Stalingrad on the Volga River, and in North Africa at El Alamein in the Egyptian desert. At the other side of the world, the Allies reconquered New Guinea.

Gandhi observed these events in his place of detention in the palace of Agha Khan near Poona. He wondered whether Allied victory was helping the cause of India. British intermediaries were in contact with him. No matter what the outcome of the war, India's fate was to be affected. In the midst of this preparatory work, on February 22, 1944, Gandhi's wife, Kasturba, in detention with him, died. They had been married for sixty-two years. Gandhi's own health was deteriorating. He contracted malaria. Finally, the British released him on May 5.

A new phase in the history of India now began. Dominion status had been promised after the war, and so the stage had to be set for this new historical phase. It was at this point that new difficulties arose which catapulted Mohammed Ali Jinnah into the forefront of events. Nehru and his companions were still in Ahmednagar Fort, but they were able to maintain contact with the Great Soul.

The situation was extremely complicated. Gandhi, Nehru, and the Congress party wanted a united India. The country constituted a natural unit, and the British had held it together during their long reign. Economically, the various parts of India were interdependent, and breaking up the country would surely jeopardize its future. But Jinnah, speaking for the Indian Muslims, demanded two countries on the subcontinent—one mainly Hindu and the other predominantly Muslim. How would the country be divided, since the Muslims did not form a homogeneous group? Their main places of settlement were a thousand miles apart, in the extreme east and extreme west near the top of India. Jinnah said the country would have two wings. The Congress leaders sought to convince him that this was not a beneficial solution. The Lean One remained adamant.

Jinnah himself was not a religious man. Yet he wanted a country in which the dominant force was the Muslim creed. He insisted that in India, Hinduism and Islam were not merely two religions but two basically different ways of life in traditions, customs, even in folkways, eating habits, and garments. There could be—he asserted—no two more different ways than these.

Nehru sized up Jinnah, an ambitious man who had worked his way up from poverty. A member of a large family in the slum section of Karachi, he had become one of the prominent barristers of the country. He, too, had had an English education in law and he, too, had come to play a leading role in the Congress party. But he could not be the leader of the party—the leader was the Great Soul. He could not even be second in rank—that was Nehru. The number-three place was carved out by Patel for himself. And Jinnah did not want to be number four. Therefore, a new country had to be made for him in which he would be number one.

There had never been a divided nation of this kind in India's history. If the Lean One had his way, what would be the Muslim country's name? Jinnah had the answer. Its name was to be Pakistan; the translation of the word is Land of the Pure. The conclusion to be drawn from that, of course, was that the bulk of the country inhabited by Hindus was not pure. Jinnah let the Hindus draw their conclusion.

This was the situation when the war was approaching its end. First, the weakest member of the Axis—Italy—was defeated. Then the formerly "invincible" German armed forces braced themselves for a last-ditch stand. Hitler was holed up in the underground redoubt of his Berlin chancellery, issuing frantic orders to his troops to stand fast. The Reich had run out of the lifeblood of modern wars— oil—and German towns were being pulverized by Allied planes. "No surrender!" Hitler raved from underground; he ordered his troops to fight until the last man fell.

On March 28, Nehru and some of his companions were transferred from Ahmednagar to Naini. From Naini, shortly thereafter, they were taken to Izatnagar Jail near Bareilly. Early in May, 1945, Germany surrendered. Japan was next.

In June, Nehru and his companions were transferred to the mountain prison of Almora. On June 15, 1945, the warden called on him. "Mr. Nehru, you are free."

Thus ended his ninth and longest term of imprisonment, one thousand and fourteen days. He was almost fifty-six years old.

Nehru spent only one night at home and then hurried to Bombay for a meeting of the Congress working committee. Next he went to the Simla conference called by the viceroy of India, the highest British official on the subcontinent.

"Though everything was familiar," Nehru noted, "and it was good to meet old friends and colleagues, I felt somewhat as a stranger and an outsider, and my mind wandered to mountains and snow-covered peaks." As soon as the Simla conference was over, he hurried to Kashmir for a rest. He did not stay in the valley but almost immediately started on a trek to the higher regions. For a month he remained in Kashmir, and then went back to the crowds and the excitement of his everyday life.

"The war ended," he wrote shortly afterward, "and the atom bomb became the symbol of the new age. The use of this bomb and the tortuous ways of power politics brought further disillusionment."

Then, hope for India began to rise.

The scene shifted to London where the great figure of Prime Minister Winston Churchill dominated the scene. Throughout the world he had been recognized as the main architect of Allied victory. It was he who had stood up to the Axis when Hitler's might appeared to be invincible.

Now Hitler was dead, presumably by his own hand, and his monstrous Third Reich of Terror was no more. In Britain, parliamentary elections were in the offing, and Churchill's victory seemed assured.

Churchill was a peacetime statesman of the old school. To him India continued to be the "diadem of the British crown" —the pivot, the heartland, the beginning and the end, the principal anchor of the imperial lifeline. With his British education, Nehru knew that, in Churchill's view, the loss of India would entail the fading away of the entire realm, and that it would affect all Britain's way of life.

Why then Nehru's hope?

Because he felt that the British might change their minds about Churchill at the forthcoming elections. He had been a great war leader, but immediately after the war the people might want a government that represented the peacetime ambitions of the English rank and file better than did the wartime titan. And Nehru knew that influential figures in the Labour party took a view of India that differed from Churchill's. Churchill would give India crumbs; Labour would hand it bread.

Many influential members of the Labour party believed that in fighting the war, Britain had lost the strength that would enable it to maintain the empire. An unhappy India would be a rebellious land. A rebellious land would have to be restrained by British arms. The people of Britain had had enough of wars and bloodshed.

India, as many Englishmen saw it, could be of greater use to Britain as a friend; a trading partner, a place for investments of money and human skills. Britain would profit by losing India—losing her as the keystone of the empire and winning her back as an ally and friend.

The British elections took place in the summer of 1945.

Churchill lost to the Labour party. The new government was headed by Clement Attlee, whom Nehru knew as a friend of India's, and an honest man with a good mind, although not spectacular or colorful. The Labour government was formed and the number-two man was Ernest Bevin, who had said that if his party won, the India Office would be closed, and its business transferred to the secretary of state for commonwealth relations. That meant independence for India. What sort of independence?

Churchill's Conservative party had now become His Majesty's Most Loyal Opposition, and it still spoke for an important segment of British public opinion. It was reinforced by a strong lobby opposed to basic changes in India's status. This lobby represented the active and retired members of the Indian Civil Service, a select group. Supremely self-confident, they believed in Britain's mission as the "little brown brethren's" guardian. Would the honest but colorless Clement Attlee stand up to Winston Churchill, a legend, and to the India lobby, a national institution? Would he be able to give India its loaf of bread?

Clement Attlee did stand up to Churchill and to the India lobby. He knew that by helping to win World War II, Britain had fallen in rank as a world power. The top world powers were now the United States and the Soviet Union, young countries on the international stage. The cold war began between East and West, and colonial powers, like Britain, were its first victims. The United States headed the "free world." How free was a world in which hundreds of millions of Indians were unfree? Working behind the scenes, America pressed the point that Britain should adjust its empire to the new age. The Soviet Union, heading the East-block countries, called upon the "downtrodden people of the world" to rise. Subject to two pressures, Britain could not have held out, even under Winston Churchill.

The cold war was not the only force pressing Britain to relinquish its imperial hold. Nehru sized up the situation very well, declaring that there could be no going back to the colonial status of India. "Gandhiji had turned liberation into a mass issue," Nehru said. "His policy of nonviolence could prevail only for a limited time." The Indian people were patient but their wrath, Nehru said, could be elemental. Nehru's man in London, Krishna Menon, was effective in transmitting these thoughts to Labour leaders. Dropping hints of what might happen should Britain wait too long, he revived memories of the Great Rebellion of 1857 in India. If there were another Great Rebellion, what would be the tragic results?

The Labour party had an ambitious domestic program to carry out. Britain was to become a better place for the working man. No longer was its land to be disfigured by industrial slums. That program would have suffered if Britain had been forced to spend its resources in fighting abroad again. The government of England made its historic decision. India was to be completely free.

At that point, however, the movement toward liberation of India ran into a new snag. The Muslim League under Mohammed Ali Jinnah stepped up its pressure for a separate country. Jinnah himself had developed a Messianic complex and assumed the title of Qaid-i-Azam, Great Leader.

Gandhi opposed the truncation of India. These were his arguments: The peninsula was a natural unit and its parts were interdependent. The subcontinent had been ruled as a single unit for generations, and the two religions, Hindu and Muslim, were living side by side. If frictions should develop, they could be removed. Goodwill and common sense would be the guides.

Nehru continued the dialogue with the Lean One. If there was a partition, said Nehru, all the people of India would suffer. Jute, a large export article, would be produced in one country, processed in the other; iron ore would be mined in one nation, turned into steel in the other. All the transportation lines would be severed; the financial connections disconnected. Independence might aggravate the peoples' plight instead of improving it. Yet, Jinnah remained undaunted.

"Do you think that we will give up our country on account of mica and burlap?" he asked.

Nehru replied, "Not on account of that alone but because India is a single unit. We prosper together or we starve separately."

Jinnah replied, "It is better to starve as an independent country, than to prosper as an Indian colony."

"All of us would be part of a united India; the Muslim League in the government . . . more heavily represented, if you wish, than its numerical weight," Nehru said.

Jinnah could not be shaken. "You are Hindus, we are Muslims, representing two ways of life, and nothing you can do will change this basic fact."

Gandhi now let Nehru do most of the work, and remained as adviser. The Mahatma, seventy-six, was too old to take an active hand in the future of the government. He remained opposed to partition, and used his unique position to create a worldwide public opinion for a united India. It was his custom to conduct religious services in the twilight hours, during which he appealed to the common sense of the people, and invoked divine aid.

Gandhi did not realize to what extent his way of life antagonized Jinnah's followers. Inadvertently, he provided a living illustration of the chasm between Hindu and Muslim. The very popularity of Gandhi irked the Muslims, because he was thought of as a prophet. To them, the last prophet had been Mohammed. The existence of the prophet Gandhi struck them as a blasphemy.

Weeks and months passed in recriminations. It was now August, 1946. August is a bad month in India because of the monsoon rains; there is either too little rain or too much. These rains begin in the spring and by August they start to get on people's nerves. Sometimes the monsoon fails, the fields become parched, and the soil turns into stone. Again nerves become frayed. In August of 1946 the nerves of many people were shattered, particularly in Calcutta.

Calcutta is the largest industrial center in India, a transportation hub near raw-material sources and markets. It is the center of Bengal province, which is inhabited by both Hindus and Muslims. Hindus make up most of the population in the west, Muslims in the east. Because Calcutta straddled these two worlds, the trouble started there.

Calcutta's factories attract countless people from the countryside. A poor monsoon season causes havoc in Bengal, and people die of famine. Many of them are too weak to fight for their lives; others, younger and more energetic, pack up their families and start the trek. They live on what they find on the way, and when they arrive in Calcutta, they are bewildered. The head of the family takes his place at the factory gate, but there is no job for him. He tries his luck anywhere that he sees a crowd; he is nearly crushed to death. Again no job. He and his family settle down to live in the gutter. Another day may bring a job. If he is lucky, he finds temporary work. But he is poorly paid; he has enough to buy cheap vegetables, but not enough for a roof. The wife and children remain at "home" in the gutter, while he is away at work, picking up leftover food from the garbage cans. They become sick but the father cannot attend to them.

In such an environment rumors spread quickly. They did in those burning August days. After a few days the young man from the countryside loses his job, and now he shares the fate of hundreds of thousands of unemployed living in the gutters. Soon he believes that he has found an explanation for why he has no work. Because he is a Muslim in a Hindu environment, and because there is no Pakistan. "Pakistan" has become a magic word that performs miracles. The young Muslim may be superstitious and feel that if there had been a Pakistan the monsoon would not have skipped his village. If there had been a Pakistan, he would have got a job in a smoke-belching, giant factory. He would be making good money, perhaps as much as a rupee a day— fifty cents. He would have food and a wonderful shelter with a roof of straw. He now has nothing because the Hindus oppose the Muslims' happiness, and ignore Jinnah.

Or the young man may be a Hindu. He feels badly that a Muslim has his job, because the Muslim is quicker in dashing through the factory gate, and gets his fabulous fifty cents a day.

The monsoon was whimsical in 1946; too little and too much. The sky was blue longer than it should have been, and then suddenly it was covered by the dark shroud of clouds; there was too much downpour in too short a time. Food prices went up. The children of many job seekers were among the famine victims. How could a father bury them?

Actually, he did not have to worry about it since there were many dead—small bodies, as well as adult ones—and by daybreak the municipal garbage trucks would scoop them up to be dumped in unmarked common graves.

Some of these hungry, jobless people started the riot. There was madness everywhere in the streets. Hindu killed Muslim, Muslim killed Hindu—for no apparent reason, except that their bitterness had turned into hatred. It was not really the monsoon's fault; it was temporary insanity. Gandhi got on the radio in a hurry. He invoked the aid of Rama, his favorite god. Nehru got on the radio, too, and talked quietly, convincingly, telling people that now their dreams were coming true, and they should not turn them into nightmares. They must show that they could organize their own country. Hindus and Muslims had lived together for many centuries and there was no reason why they should not continue to do so, now that they had their great chance. India's great men spoke in vain. The blood of Muslims tainted the hands of Hindus, and Hindu blood was shed by Muslims; first in Bengal, then in the provinces of Bihar and elsewhere. The British hastened to transfer power to India. The longer the negotiations, the greater the danger of more bloodshed.

In spite of Gandhi's opposition, the Congress leaders now had to resign themselves to partition. There would be two nations on the subcontinent, in three parts. There was to be India, of course, and there was to be also Pakistan, with its two wings separated by a thousand miles of Indian territory. Pakistan and India retained large minorities of the other's people. A tenth of Pakistan's population was Hindu and a tenth of India's Muslim. Thus both retained major problems. Besides the communal problem, there were the

five hundred and sixty-two princely states. What was to be
their fate? Some were no more than clusters of villages;
others were very large. For instance, one princely state
had more than sixteen million inhabitants on a territory of
eighty-two thousand miles—a sizable country. This country
was ruled by the Nizam of Hyderabad, Sir Osman Ali Khan.
His wealth had been estimated at two billion dollars and he
had some ten thousand retainers. What was to happen to
him?

There was no time to negotiate detailed separate agreements. Britain washed its hands of the princely states. It
would have been absurd to have hundreds of Pakistans and
Indias. The princes would have to reach agreements with
the new nations; they would have to join one or the other.
They were to receive yearly payments from the new countries.
The Nizam of Hyderabad was forced into joining India,
and he was given a yearly allowance of one million dollars.
In years to come he would complain that he was a charity
case. Also in years to come his one hundred and twenty
sons (from many marriages) formed a "brothers' brother-
hood," to force their father to raise their allowance from
thirty dollars a month to ninety.

∽ NINE ∾

Independence and a Bullet

On August 15, 1947, the Dominion of India was created, and Jawaharlal Nehru, the fifty-seven-year-old Brahman from Kashmir, became its first prime minister. It was to be the world's most populated democratic country.

Prime Minister Nehru, elegant as always, with the inseparable rosebud in his buttonhole, delivered his inaugural speech at the first session of the first parliament of India in the capital city of New Delhi. "Long years ago we made a tryst with destiny, and now the time comes when we shall redeem our pledge. . . . A moment comes which occurs but rarely in history, when we step out from the old to the

183

new, when an age ends, and when the soul of a nation, long suppressed, finds utterance.

"At this moment I think . . . of what took place at the making of the great American nation when the fathers of that country met and fashioned a Constitution which stood the test of so many years, more than a century and a half, and of the great nation which has resulted, built up on the basis of that Constitution."

Nehru thus selected the United States as the model of his nation, and so he continued:

"So our mind goes back to these great examples and we seek to learn from their success to avoid failures because some measure of failure is inherent in all human effort. Nevertheless, we shall advance, I am certain, in spite of obstruction and difficulties, and achieve and realize the dream that we have dreamt so long."

There were obstructions and difficulties indeed, right at the outset. One of the first materialized in the very Kashmir region from which the Nehru clan descended. The Kashmir problem was to haunt the new nation and its Pakistani neighbor for many years.

Some 80 per cent of the population of Kashmir was Muslim. However, its ruler, Maharaja Sir Hari Singh Bahadur, was a Hindu. He also happened to be something of a playboy. As we have seen, the act of independence provided that in the case of each of the princely states, its ruler had to decide on the question of joining India or Pakistan, or—in an exceptional case—remaining unattached. Kashmir was adjacent to both countries, and it was large. The maharaja decided that he preferred to be left alone. That was not, however, the wish of Pakistan, which took a deep interest in the mainly Muslim people of the mountainous principality. Suddenly, tribesmen appeared in Kashmir, coming from the direction of Pakistan. The government of that country, in the city of Karachi, claimed that this was a spontaneous uprising for which it was not responsible. After a while, regular Pakistani army units joined the tribesmen. Faced with the possibility of being drowned in a Muslim tidal wave, the maharaja decided to change his position, and he sent his pledge of accession to Nehru.

Promptly, the New Delhi government dispatched its airborne troops which occupied as much territory as they could, including about three-fourths of the population. The best part of Kashmir, comprising the beautiful valley with the capital of Srinagar, was now in Indian hands. Legally, Kashmir's fate was decided by the ruler's accession act. He himself faded out of the picture within a short time, and that should have settled the matter. But Nehru, in a burst of generosity, and perhaps also with a view toward avoiding future arguments on this issue, declared that the ultimate destiny of the mountain state would be decided in a plebiscite, after the occupation troops had been withdrawn. The troops were not withdrawn by either side, and the plebiscite did not take place. Pakistan took the case to the United Nations for the first time immediately after these events and then many times afterward. The problem has become a perennial. Eventually, India completely incorporated Kashmir, leaving no chance for a plebiscite.

Nehru insisted on retaining Kashmir, some observers said, because of his own family background. That was probably not the reason. Public opinion in India was savagely against Pakistan after India's incorporation of Kashmir. Once the Vale of Kashmir was under Hindu rule, it became impossible to transfer it to the detested neighbor. Nehru came to fear

a plebiscite for another reason, too. Should the Kashmiri
vote for Pakistan, there was danger that India's tens of
millions of Muslims would become the victims of the ex-
tremist Hindus' hatred. The Kashmir issue turned out to
be a calamity for all concerned.

Then tragedy struck, not once but twice, inaugurating an
age of tears. The dream turned into a nightmare.

Even before the declaration of independence there had
been violence between Hindus and Muslims. Now that
partition had become a reality, millions were gripped by
panic. The Hindus in areas assigned to Pakistan dreaded
their new Muslim masters, while the Muslims of India
feared their Hindu neighbors' wrath. There was really no
reason for this fear, which was caused by uncertainty, poverty,
the trying climate, and apprehension about the future. Millions left their huts and gutters, away from their old neighbors of a different creed. They set out toward the great
unknown, hoping to find a new hut or a new place in the
gutters behind the boundaries of the nation which professed
their own creed.

The Hindus were on the move; the Muslims were on the
move. In between them—in and near the Punjab—the Sikhs,
fearing both sides, were also on the move. How many of
them filled the roads? Nobody could count the miserable
refugees. Estimates ran as high as fourteen million.

When Hindu and Muslim caravans met, they clashed and
their members started to slaughter one another. Loot was
not their object because all of them were beggars. They did
this out of unreasoning hatred, and thus the two countries
were launched on a tidal wave of blood. The number of the
dead victims remained unknown, too. It may have been a
million.

Gandhi, now an old man, went among the people, pleading with them. And so did Nehru.

"For years we were working to make India free," the prime minister told his people. "Many people in our ranks suffered martyrdom, rotting in noisome jails. You, the people, sustained us with your resolve to win and we have reached the threshold of a new era. This should be our turn to demonstrate our maturity, since this is the moment for which we were waiting. And what is happening now? Instead of clasping our neighbors to our bosoms, many of you are strangling them. Our country has been conceived in the spirit of *Gandiji,* which is nonviolence. We had earned the world's respect because we gained our freedom by peaceful means. Why this insensate outburst against fellow-sufferers? Draw back; it is not too late to stay the fratricidal hand. All of us are brothers, in suffering and hope. In the name of our cause, stop this murder! Heed the words of *Gandhiji,* our teacher, and do not besmirch our noble cause with blood!"

Eventually, the massacre ended because of exhaustion. But this was not yet the end of the tragedy.

Gandhi observed these awful events with profound sorrow. This was not the kind of independence he had wanted. He told his countrymen, on January 13, 1948, that he would fast unto death to induce the end of communal violence. As he had many times before, he led an open-air prayer meeting in New Delhi on the thirtieth of the month. Hindu extremists were furious because he wanted to save Muslim lives. One of them, a former member of the reactionary Mahasabha which fought partition, stole close to the spot where Gandhi was sitting. Taking careful aim and uttering a prayer that his bullet might hit its mark, he fired three times at Gandhi.

188 JAWAHARLAL NEHRU

The Great Soul had only time to gasp, *"Hé Ram"* ("Oh God").

Horror swept not only the crowd of worshipers but also the entire world. The British statesman who had tried to solve the Indian problem, Sir Stafford Cripps, said: "I know no other man of any time . . . who so forcefully and convincingly demonstrated the power of spirit over material things."

"Friends and comrades," said Gandhi's disciple Nehru, "the light has gone out of our lives and there is darkness everywhere."

∾ TEN ∾

"Mr. India" and the Darshana

The house on Teen Murti Marg, into which Nehru moved as prime minister, had been the residence of the commanders of the British armed forces in India. Now it became the powerhouse of the country. Nehru worked at least fourteen hours a day, seven days a week.

He rose early, after only five or six hours' sleep, and took his yoga exercises, which included standing on his head. He put on his white jodphurs, loose as far as the knee and tight below. When going out, he wore his white cap. Sometimes he went horseback riding or swimming. Then back to the

189

house for breakfast; his favorite was pancakes and syrup, the main item on the menu.

By that time visitors were assembled in the spacious garden. It was well kept, filled with flowers and trees. It was also stocked with a few favorite animals for the children —cuddly pandas, tiger cubs, monkeys, and a tiny crocodile. The garden was a delight to youngsters, especially his own grandchildren, Indira's two sons.

The people who waited for Nehru presented petitions or brought contributions for the victims of calamities—so frequent in India—or they just wanted to look at him to be exposed to his blessed presence.

Nehru was one of India's great sights, like the Taj Mahal. He was always elegant and polite. Always he wore a rosebud in his buttonhole. He was never loud, trivial, or gossipy. But he could show his displeasure. When he was bored by people he tapped his fingers and looked at the ceiling. His associates knew that when he projected his lower lip, he was angry.

Nehru never remarried, and the hostess of the prime minister's residence was his daughter, Indira. He was closer to her than to any other human being. It almost seemed as if he wanted to make amends through her for his neglect of the other women in his family.

As a hostess, Indira had few peers. She looked after all his needs in the spacious mansion of Teen Murti Marg; inspected the menu; and always had the daily rosebud for his buttonhole. She saw to it, too, that her father had time to play with Rajiv and Sanjay, her sons.

Indira was still fascinated by politics, not as a diversion but as a subject of deep interest. Her father discovered that she had "high-fidelity reception" when meeting people. She could distinguish between reality and its imitation, between the natural and artificial in the way people talked, looked, and established contact. Indira's reactions to people were useful, and Nehru took her along on his diplomatic trips. She was with him when he met the Chinese Communist leaders in Bandung, Indonesia, in the spring of 1955. She accompanied him on his visit to Yugoslavia's Tito, and to the leaders in Moscow. She talked little, but listened carefully.

Jokingly, Nehru remarked, "Those big eyes of hers soak up every word. My brains forget; her eyes remember." And more than that, as he admitted to a confidant in a moment of relaxation, "I have seen many people in my life, and have been a witness to too much dissimulation and sometimes my intuition fails. She has young, healthy reactions."

In playful moods, Nehru teased his daughter. "I am only minister for external affairs, indeed, very external. You are minister of the internal affairs of the external affairs, and that is the real ministry."

Indira became a prominent figure in Indian politics. Friends persuaded her to accept an appointment as a member of the Congress party's powerful twenty-one-member working committee, which passes on all major candidates and platform planks. "Indira jeeped and flew to every corner of the country," an American periodical reported, "going to villages that had never before been visited by outsiders, much less by someone as important as Nehru's daughter."

Nehru's daughter was particularly interested in the welfare of children. She served as the president of the Indian Council of Child Welfare; as the vice-president of the International Union of Child Welfare; as a member of the

Indian delegation to UNESCO, the United Nations' body
dealing with education and other subjects; and she subsequently became a member of the executive board of the same
organization, and of its central advisory board on education.
She also served as chairman of the National Integration
Committee of the Indian National Congress; worked for
the National Institute of Women; for the institute named
after her mother, Kamala Nehru Vidayalaya; for the Bal
Bhawan (Children's Home); Bal Sahyog (Children's
Cooperative); and other social welfare organizations.

In later years she served on the executive committee of
the National Defense Fund. In 1959, she served as president
of the Indian National Congress party, following in the
footsteps of her grandfather and father. She became minister
of information and broadcasting in the Indian government.
She did not forget her Himalayan ancestry, either: she became
a member of the governing body of the Himalayan Moun-
taineering Institute, and worked for the Tibetan Homes
Foundation.

Her fame spread far and wide. In the United States she
was honored in a variety of ways. Among many honors
conferred upon her was the Howland Memorial Prize of
Yale University. She was the recipient, in 1953, of the
Mothers' Award in the United States. Some years later, she
was named one of the three greatest women in the contemporary world.

Her work aroused much admiration, and considerable
jealousy.

"Are we going to have a royal succession? Is Indira going
to be our Queen Elizabeth?" some people in India fretted.

The grumblers were, however, in a minority. Many leaders

found Indira's work for her father helpful. They talked to Nehru about it.

"Indira has a favorable image in the country. She should be more closely linked to our party."

"True enough," he answered, "but—"

He reminded them that another Nehru, his older sister, already occupied a prominent position in the country.

"I don't want Congress to feel that we Nehrus have a monopoly on government posts."

Indeed, his own sister Swarup occupied important posts in the government of India. The world knew her better as Madame Pandit, and she was admired for her ability as well as for her attractive looks. She had been the first woman minister in a provincial government—under British rule, a decade before independence. Then she became minister of local self-government and public health in the United Provinces. After independence, she rose still higher to become, successively, ambassador to the Soviet Union, ambassador to the United States, and president of the General Assembly of the United Nations.

Nehru's objections against having too many members of his family in politics were answered in this way: "Panditji, is it your fault that your family has produced such able people?"

The prime minister was truly India's powerhouse. On an average day, he received five hundred letters and one hundred telegrams. He had interviews and conferences with subordinates, dignitaries, and foreign celebrities. When parliament was in session, he was on hand, moving from the Lok Sabha (House of the People) to the Rajya Sabha (Council of States), making policy declarations, and answering questions on a large variety of subjects. His statements were so well formulated that they could be printed without revision.

He combined and performed the most important functions of the government: prime minister, minister of external affairs, minister for atomic energy, and occasionally minister of defense. As chairman of the planning commission, he was also in charge of the national economy. He produced an incredible amount of work—too much, his critics said. He *was* the state machinery, and what if he broke down?

Serene and staid on the surface, internally Nehru was in a rush—there was so much to do and so little time. He had to see to it that India's people had enough to eat, that they lived longer, that their children went to school, that the country pulled its weight in foreign affairs.

When he took over the government, the average life expectancy in India was twenty-nine years (as compared to more than twice that in the Western world). More than half of India's children died before reaching their fifth birthday; more than 80 per cent of the people could neither read nor write; millions died each year in epidemics; and when the monsoons failed, millions died of starvation.

Food was the first item on Nehru's agenda—food for India. How to speed up its production? If left to the traditional ways of the peasants, production would remain low.

More irrigation was needed for millions of arid acres. Above all, hydroelectric power stations would have to be built. Fertilizers were needed to revive the tired soil. More security was needed for the peasant; landlords had to be prevented from overcharging him. Nehru knew that land reform was needed, too. The government would have to buy up land from the estate owners and sell it to landless peasants in a pay-as-you-work plan. But that was for the future.

India needed more industries. Manufacturing plants could produce the articles at home—at cheaper prices—which India now had to buy abroad at high prices. But manufacturing plants required big machines, and these were costly. Also few local capitalists had enough money to invest, and even fewer were willing to risk it on ventures that did not promise quick returns.

More roads had to be built to enable help to come quickly during national emergencies—drought, flood, or famine. More low-cost housing was needed, too—not merely for millions but for hundreds of millions.

Now that India was no longer a dependency, people expected changes to occur promptly and miraculously. For years they had lulled themselves into the belief that independence automatically meant more food, health, schools, and happiness. Therefore, the great hurry. India was one of the poorest countries in the world. Dividing the value of all the goods and services produced in one year (the GNP— gross national product) by the number of all inhabitants, the yearly income per person amounted to only forty dollars at the time of independence.

How could quick results be achieved? Nehru felt it could best be done by organizing production, assigning high priorities to the most important items. Therefore, India started on its Five-Year Plans, combining the production of private and public sectors, and aided by other countries that recognized the Nehru government's need for outside help. If Indians' expectations were not fulfilled, they might turn to communism to produce quick results but . . . at what cost!

The Western nations, especially the United States, did not want this to happen.

The health of India had to improve, too, and quickly. Schools had to be built. New universities and research institutions had to be opened.

As a result of planning and hard work, production increased, health improved, and more schools were established. Then came the population explosion. The estimated population of the country on Independence Day was 340,000,000. Twenty years later it was 500,000,000. The food supply had been overtaken by the population growth, as had been predicted many years before by Thomas Malthus, the English economist. In production figures, the Five-Year Plans succeeded, but in relative figures they failed. After three Five-Year Plans, the life span in India reached forty-seven years. But 100,000,000 Indians were not fully employed and of these 20,000,000 were not employed at all.

How well did Nehru succeed in foreign affairs? He was dedicated to peace, as Gandhi had been. To Nehru, war in a world replete with nuclear weapons was insanity. All controversies, he held, could be solved by tact and common sense.

Yet Kashmir, his own ancestral land, was bristling with arms. And after India became independent, Portugal still retained the colony of Goa, a toehold on India's western coast. Nehru wanted the Portuguese out, but they refused to budge. On a December day in 1961, Indian armies moved into Goa and dislodged the Portuguese. Nehru solved the Goa problem but not by peaceful means.

In 1962, China drove up to the crest of the Himalayas, claiming boundaries that India refused to recognize. Nehru's government moved up armed forces in order to halt the

Chinese. In this instance again Nehru did not turn his other cheek. Arms were to decide the issue, not Gandhi's satyagraha.

For a time Nehru's India appeared to be the pivot of the so-called Third-Force nations, uncommitted to either side in the East-West disputes. He, more than any other leader of the Third-Force countries, was recognized as the conscience of humanity.

At the same time, India's disputes with other countries— in Kashmir, Goa, and along the Chinese frontier—were causes of deep concern to Nehru. The Brahman who had wanted to make a unique record for himself as a man of peace became embroiled in wars which compromised his standing as the spokesman of the uncommitted world.

Yet Nehru still thought of war as an absurdity, and the denial of human dignity. Killing and being killed denied man's divine image. Wars were waged by armies which called for regimentation. Dignity and regimentation, he believed, were incompatibles. Besides, wars created more problems than they solved. The worst enemy of peace, in his view, was the "fatalism of war," the belief that it was inevitable—the only solution among nations.

"There has developed a fatalistic tendency," he said, "to think in terms of war. Yet, the prospect of war is so bad and its consequences so evil that I want every human being to try his utmost to avoid it."

But how could he foster the desire for peace?

"If we want peace," he said, "we must develop the temper of peace and . . . understand others just as we expect them to understand us."

And during his visit to the United States he made this remark to a large group in New York: "We have not got

an atom bomb. And if I may say so, I rejoice in not having
the atom bomb."

After the death of the Great Soul, Nehru felt very much
alone except for the comforting presence of Indira. He was
strong and sturdy, but he had reached the "dangerous age."
He had been Gandhi's crown prince but did Nehru himself
have an heir?

The Congress party could not seem to generate new blood.
Maybe it was too old, too much of a monopoly. The highest
places were occupied by deeply entrenched members who
wanted no change. Perhaps the younger people were turning
away from the Congress to more radical creeds—communism,
socialism, or super-patriotism. Or perhaps the younger generation was just not going into politics. Why should they? What
was the use? The old guard was too strong and could not be
dislodged.

However, there were some gifted people in the old guard,
too. An administrative genius, Vallabhbhai Patel was considered India's number-two man. Patel was the businessmen's
friend, a conservative—as conservative as Nehru was liberal.
Gandhi had put Patel in his strong position. "He is pure as
crystal, truthful beyond suspicion," the Great Soul used to
say about Patel, this favorite disciple. "The nation is safe in
his hands." But Patel died two years after Gandhi. Who had
become the number-two man?

Was it Krishna Menon? He had helped Nehru in London
and had stood beside him when some of the Congress stalwarts tried to demote him. The prime minister felt attracted
to Menon and they shared many ideas: both were socialists
and strongly opposed to fascism and other forms of the right.
Menon knew his way in diplomacy, too. He was endowed
with an inventive mind and much energy. But he was too

testy; he was disliked in America and he was not too popular in Britain, either.

Public opinion in India followed the work of another Congress stalwart, Morarji Desai, an efficient financier who ran the government's economy for a while. He knew how to capture newspaper headlines, but he was too pushy, or so Nehru thought. The Bombay political leader, S.K. Patil, was a man of much energy, and he was held in high esteem by the business community of India. Nehru got along with Patil fairly well, but did not trust his political views. Y.B. Chavan, who became the country's minister of defense at the time of the boundary crisis with China, had too much of a "computer mind" for Nehru's tastes.

It was said of Nehru that he was like a banyan tree, providing shadow for a large number of politicians who carried on their shady trade. Many of them did not have the ability to carry on the nation's business, but they felt entitled to high positions because of their oratorical gifts. So, no adequate successor seemed to be in sight.

The years passed, and few of India's great expectations materialized. Yet the country remained fairly quiet. Nehru stood at the head of state, and the people trusted him. Nearly all the new countries born after World War II turned to one-party rule, often headed by military men. India remained a democracy, perhaps the only one in the underdeveloped world. That it did so was an achievement attributed solely to Nehru, recognized the world over as "Mr. India."

He kept his finger on the pulse of India. He traveled all over the country, addressing the peasants to whom he was much attracted. Contact with the people rejuvenated him. They came from all over to hear him, and they listened with rapt attention. Although his Cambridge-trained speech was foreign to their ears, that did not matter. What did matter was his darshana, as much a blessing as the sacred Ganges.

But Nehru was getting tired. The number of problems was so vast that no human could solve them. Gradually, he became too weary to face the countless issues. For the same reason, he "developed a blind eye," in the words of P. H. Pathwardan, the eminent Indian scholar, "for the glaring faults and misconducts of his colleagues in high places."

Nehru's eyes were still keen even though his energies were increasingly dissipated. With the capacity to see himself in perspective, he saw that much more should have been done, and he hoped that his people's trust might recharge him with new dynamism. Because he did hold the trust of his people he could not relinquish the helm. The words of the famed American poet Robert Frost helped Nehru to face bravely tomorrow's work. Four lines of a Frost poem were constantly at Nehru's bedside:

> The woods are lovely, dark and deep,
> But I have promises to keep,
> And miles to go before I sleep,
> And miles to go before I sleep.

Because Nehru felt a great responsibility toward India— toward the people, and not just the land—he also felt that he could not afford to sleep. In his will drawn up a decade before his death, he expressed this sense of dedication.

"I have received so much love and affection from the Indian people that nothing I can do can repay even a small fraction of it, and, indeed, there can be no repayment of so precious a thing as affection."

There was another aspect of Nehru's character, too. He

became young again in the company of children. To them he was Chacha Nehru—Uncle Nehru. "For a moment I forget," he wrote, "that I am terribly old and that it is a very long time ago since I was a child."

This was part of his uniqueness, that he did not look old even when he was, and that he could still play with children. He was happy to show them his favorite pandas and the lively tiger cub in the garden of his mansion. He always liked to play with the cub—but first he put on heavy gloves.

Should Nehru have resigned in 1958 as the scholar Pathwardan suggested? It was true that the old energy and drive had deserted him. But how could he desert the people of India when they believed that he, and he alone, had the "blessed presence"? He was the number-one man, and there was no one else. According to Pathwardan, Nehru had become totally passive by 1961, and the ruling Congress party "colorless and flabby." Finally, Nehru intimated to the party that he wanted to move out of the limelight. The answer was an unconditional no. He was, after all, Mr. India.

Nehru had always thought that there was no limit to his strength. Then he had a stroke in January, 1964, which left him partly paralyzed for a time. While his powers of recovery were strong, he did look tired and wan, and had to cut back his heavy load of work. Once again he recalled Frost's poem:

And miles to go before I sleep,
And miles to go before I sleep.

After the stroke there were no more miles, only yards, and then inches. He was seventy-four years old when he had his final stroke, at 2 P.M., on May 27, 1964, the "sleep." In

death there were hardly any wrinkles on his face. He looked
less doleful than in life, and some people detected just a
shadow of a smile around his lips. India was stunned as the
public media announced: "*Panditji* is no more."

He lay in state at the prime minister's residence. His
daughter sat at the foot of the bier. Then came the farewell;
the funeral cortege, millions flanking the route, to the funeral
pyre at Shanti Ghat in New Delhi, on May 28. His grandson
Sanjay ignited the pyre, while the strains of the chant rose
toward the sky: "Abide With Me," then, "Lead, Kindly
Light."

These words came from President Johnson of the United
States:

"For so long we had counted on his influence for good; it
now seems impossible to believe that he is no longer with
us. . . . His passing has left his country and all mankind,
to whom he gave so much in word and deed, the poorer.
. . . Perhaps more than any other world leader, he has given
expression to man's yearning for peace."

From the underdeveloped countries came this word, expressed by the prime minister of Kenya, Joma Kenyatta:
". . . His name will be remembered forever throughout the
world."

Nehru wanted a handful of his ashes to be cast into the
Ganges River. "The Ganga [Ganges] has been a symbol of
India's age-long culture and civilization," he had written in
his will, "ever-changing, ever-flowing and yet ever the same
Ganga. . . . As my last homage to India's cultural inheri-
tance I am making this request that a handful of my ashes be
thrown into the Ganga at Allahabad to be carried to the great
ocean that washes India's shores."

His epitaph, which he himself composed, summarized his dreams and deeds:

"This was the man, who with all his mind and heart, loved India and the Indian people. And they, in turn, were indulgent to him and gave him of their love abundantly and extravagantly."

His spirit animated the work of his successor, Lal Bahadur Shastri, a former associate and Congress party secretary, who defined his goal in these words: "Let us bend ourselves to the great task before us—an India free, prosperous and strong, and a world at peace—these would be the most fitting memorials to Gandhiji and Jawaharlal."

It was in the spirit of these two immortals of history that Shastri negotiated peace with India's neighbor Pakistan, when death overtook him on January 11, 1966. The search was now on for a successor—a worthy heir to Nehru. Should it be Desai, Chavan, or, perhaps, Menon? It was none of these. The choice fell on the "crown princess," Indira, Nehru's companion and only child. And that, no doubt, because of the radiance of the father, and the grandfather, too—the family aura. A woman was to be the prime minister in a country of five hundred million people, many of them tradition-bound, with a traditional bias against women.

Indira faced a severe test after the 1967 nationwide elections in which the Congress party lost its unquestioned supremacy, while retaining its majority in the New Delhi legislature. The election results were followed by much heart searching. Was Indira the right person for the grueling job? No other candidate could win a consensus. After all, Indira had the aura and the Nehru family was a patented and even sanctified institution. While the National Congress party lost much, Indira Gandhi, the daughter of the immortal Jawaharlal, granddaughter of the celebrated Motilal, came out ahead. Inevitably, her status would change, but not yet. India was holding on to Jawaharlal's magic mantle.

Whatever the fate of the daughter, the name of the father was enshrined in history. Jawaharlal Nehru was advanced to the position of a prophet, whose every deed was enshrined in print; whose anniversaries became causes for festivities. Institutions of many kinds were named after him. The Jawaharlal Nehru University bill, for instance, provided for the establishment of a school of higher learning in New Delhi to "promote the study of the principles for which Nehru lived and worked." His residence in the nation's capital, in which he had tried to lay the foundation of a modern India, became the Nehru Museum and Library, dedicated to his life and deeds.

Other countries, too, paid homage to the Nehru name. Britain remembered the man with particular affection—the same England he loved and fought. Trinity College, Cambridge, his alma mater, established the Nehru Memorial Lecture Series to perpetuate recollection of his imperishable deeds. It was a Master of Trinity College, Lord Butler, a former leading light of the Conservative party—with which Nehru had no affinity—who on the anniversary of Nehru's death summarized history's verdict.

"At the bar of history, Nehru will emerge as a great Indian and a great world figure, not unscathed perhaps, but as a man whose contribution to the cause of effective democracy ranks as high as those Himalayan mountain peaks which towered above his erstwhile prison walls."

~ ELEVEN ~

Words of Jawaharlal Nehru

How amazing is this spirit of man! In spite of innumerable failings, man, throughout the ages, has sacrificed his life and all he held dear for an ideal, for truth, for faith, for country and honor. That ideal may change, but that capacity for self-sacrifice continues, and because of that, much may be forgiven to man, and it is impossible to lose hope for him.

True freedom is not merely political, but must also be economic and spiritual. Only with this combination can man grow and fulfil his destiny.

It is dangerous and harmful to be guided in our life's course by hatreds and aversions, for they are wasteful of energy and limit and twist the mind and prevent it from perceiving the truth.

We have definitely accepted the democratic process . . . because we think that in the final analysis it promotes the growth of human beings and of society. . . . It is not enough for us, merely to produce the material goods of the world. We do want high standards of living, but not at the cost of man's creative spirit . . . not at the cost of all those fine things of life which have ennobled man throughout the ages.

Peace cannot be purchased by compromise with evil or by surrender to it. Nor can peace be maintained by methods that themselves are the negation of peace.

When we talked of the independence of India it was not in terms of isolation. We realized, perhaps more than many other countries, that the old type of complete national independence was doomed and there must be a new era of world co-operation. . . .

I have no doubt in my mind that World Government must and will come, for there is no other remedy for the world's sickness.

The cultured mind, rooted in itself, should have its doors and windows open. It should have the capacity to understand the other's viewpoint fully even though it cannot always agree with it.

The call of action stirs strange depths within me and, after a brief tussle with thought, I want to experience again "that *lonely* impulse of delight" which turns to risk and danger and faces and mocks at death.

Once I was asked, "What is your principal problem? How many problems have you got?" I said, "We have got 360 million problems in India." Now that answer amused people, but it has an essential truth in it.

A nation does not die. Men and women come and go, but the nation goes on. It has something of the eternal about it. And India certainly is that type of nation which has something of eternity behind it, in its ideas and in its growth, and even in its decay. So we shall pass, and the burden that we have carried, adequately or not, will fall on other shoulders.

CHRONOLOGY

1889   Jawaharlal Nehru, son of Motilal Nehru and Swaruprani, born in Allahabad, India, on November 14.

1900   Swarup, his sister, born.

1905   Taken to England; enters Harrow, boys' preparatory schoool.

1907   Graduates from Harrow; enters Trinity College, Cambridge.

1907   Krishna, his sister, born.

1910   Graduates from Cambridge; enters Inner Temple, law school in London.

1912   Passes bar examination; returns to India.

1913   Begins law practice in Allahabad.

1916   Marries Shrimati Kamala Kaul in Delhi; meets Gandhi for the first time.

1917   Indira, the Nehrus' only surviving child, is born.

1919   He and father, Motilal, join Gandhi actively after the Jallianwallah Bagh massacre in Amritsar.

1920   Turns to the reform movement of the Indian National Congress party.

1921   Imprisoned for the first time, in Lucknow, during civil-disobedience campaign against British.

1922   Released from Lucknow District Jail on March 3;
       rearrested on May 11, second term; released in
       August, he is jailed again in October, and sentenced
       to six months.

1923   Released from jail; elected secretary of All-India
       Congress Committee; arrested by authorities of
       Nabha princely state and sentenced to 2½ years;
       serves only a few days and is released on condition
       that he leaves the state.

1926–27 Visits Europe with family; back in India, addresses
       forty-second session of Indian National Congress.

1929   Elected president of Congress.

1930   Jailed and sentenced to six months for breaking
       the salt law on April 5—his fourth term in jail;
       released in October; jailed again the same month
       and sentenced to two years.

1931   Released.

1932   Jailed again and resentenced to two years, January
       4.

1933   Released from prison on August 30.

1934   Tours Bihar province after earthquake; jailed on
       sedition charge and sentenced to two years—his
       seventh prison term.

1935   Released because of his wife's health; visits wife in
       European sanatorium.

1936   Wife dies February 28 in Swiss sanatorium; Nehru
       flies back to India; reelected president of Congress.

1937   Reelected president of Congress.

1938   Tours Europe for six months; visits Spain during
       civil war.

1939   Visits Ceylon and China.

1940   Jailed because of renewed civil-disobedience campaign.

1941   Released from prison, December 4.

1942   Takes part in negotiations with Sir Stafford Cripps; jailed because of Quit India Manifesto—his ninth, longest, and last jail term; Indira marries Feroze Gandhi, March 26.

1945   Released from jail on June 15.

1946   Elected president of Congress for fourth term; forms provisional government.

1947   August 15, Independence Day; Nehru elected first prime minister of independent nation; encounters Kashmir problem and riots.

1948   Gandhi is assassinated on January 30.

1949   Nehru arrives in the United States.

1950   India becomes republic January 26; Nehru reelected prime minister.

1951   First Five-Year Plan.

1951–54 Elected president of Indian National Congress party.

1956   Presents second Five-Year Plan to parliament.

1960   Addresses United Nations General Assembly in New York.

1961   Orders occupation of Goa, Portuguese enclave in India; presents third Five-Year Plan.

1962   Leads Congress party to victory in nationwide elections; India and China in armed clash over borders.

1963   Government and Congress party reorganized.

1964   Dies in New Delhi on May 27 at the age of seventy-four.

BIBLIOGRAPHY

SELECTED BOOKS BY NEHRU:

The Discovery of India. New York: John Day, 1946.
The First Sixty Years. Selected and edited by Dorothy Nor-
man. New York: John Day, 1965. (Selections of the
writings, speeches, statements, press conferences, conversa-
tions, interviews, etc., of Jawaharlal Nehru.)
India's Freedom. London: George Allen & Unwin, 1962.
Nehru on Gandhi. New York: John Day, 1948.
Nehru on World History, condensed by Saul K. Padover.
New York: John Day, 1960.
Nehru's Letters to His Sister. London: Faber & Faber, 1963.
Toward Freedom. New York: John Day, 1942.
Visit to America. New York: John Day, 1950.

SELECTED BOOKS ABOUT NEHRU:

Brecher, Michael. *Nehru, a Political Biography.* New York:
Oxford University Press, 1959.
Crocker, Walter Russell. *Nehru: A Contemporary Estimate.*
New York: Oxford University Press, 1966.

Das, Manmath Nath. *The Political Philosophy of Jawaharlal Nehru.* New York: John Day, 1961.

Hutheesing, Krishna Nehru, with Alden Hatch. *We Nehrus.* New York: Holt, Rinehart and Winston, 1967.

Mohan, Anand. *Indira Gandhi: A Personal and Political Biography.* New York: Meredith Press, 1967.

Moraes, Frank. *Jawaharlal Nehru.* New York: Macmillan, 1956.

Nanda, Bal Ram. *The Nehrus: Motilal and Jawaharlal.* New York: John Day, 1963.

Sahgal, Nayantara. *Prison and Chocolate Cake.* New York: Knopf, 1954.

Sharma Jagdish Saran. *Jawaharlal Nehru: A Descriptive Bibliography.* Delhi: Chand & Company, 1955.

Smith, Donald Eugene. *Nehru and Democracy: The Political Thought of an Asian Democrat.* Bombay: Orient Longmanns, 1958.

INDEX

213